C-4557   CAREER EXAMINATION SERIES

*This is your*
*PASSBOOK for...*

# Water Utility Worker

*Test Preparation Study Guide*
*Questions & Answers*

# COPYRIGHT NOTICE

This book is SOLELY intended for, is sold ONLY to, and its use is RESTRICTED to individual, bona fide applicants or candidates who qualify by virtue of having seriously filed applications for appropriate license, certificate, professional and/or promotional advancement, higher school matriculation, scholarship, or other legitimate requirements of education and/or governmental authorities.

This book is NOT intended for use, class instruction, tutoring, training, duplication, copying, reprinting, excerption, or adaptation, etc., by:

1) Other publishers
2) Proprietors and/or Instructors of "Coaching" and/or Preparatory Courses
3) Personnel and/or Training Divisions of commercial, industrial, and governmental organizations
4) Schools, colleges, or universities and/or their departments and staffs, including teachers and other personnel
5) Testing Agencies or Bureaus
6) Study groups which seek by the purchase of a single volume to copy and/or duplicate and/or adapt this material for use by the group as a whole without having purchased individual volumes for each of the members of the group
7) Et al.

Such persons would be in violation of appropriate Federal and State statutes.

PROVISION OF LICENSING AGREEMENTS – Recognized educational, commercial, industrial, and governmental institutions and organizations, and others legitimately engaged in educational pursuits, including training, testing, and measurement activities, may address request for a licensing agreement to the copyright owners, who will determine whether, and under what conditions, including fees and charges, the materials in this book may be used them.  In other words, a licensing facility exists for the legitimate use of the material in this book on other than an individual basis.  However, it is asseverated and affirmed here that the material in this book CANNOT be used without the receipt of the express permission of such a licensing agreement from the Publishers.  Inquiries re licensing should be addressed to the company, attention rights and permissions department.

All rights reserved, including the right of reproduction in whole or in part, in any form or by any means, electronic or mechanical, including photocopying, recording, or by any information storage and retrieval system, without permission in writing from the Publisher.

Copyright © 2024 by
## National Learning Corporation

212 Michael Drive, Syosset, NY 11791
(516) 921-8888 • www.passbooks.com
E-mail: info@passbooks.com

# PASSBOOK® SERIES

THE *PASSBOOK® SERIES* has been created to prepare applicants and candidates for the ultimate academic battlefield – the examination room.

At some time in our lives, each and every one of us may be required to take an examination – for validation, matriculation, admission, qualification, registration, certification, or licensure.

Based on the assumption that every applicant or candidate has met the basic formal educational standards, has taken the required number of courses, and read the necessary texts, the *PASSBOOK® SERIES* furnishes the one special preparation which may assure passing with confidence, instead of failing with insecurity. Examination questions – together with answers – are furnished as the basic vehicle for study so that the mysteries of the examination and its compounding difficulties may be eliminated or diminished by a sure method.

This book is meant to help you pass your examination provided that you qualify and are serious in your objective.

The entire field is reviewed through the huge store of content information which is succinctly presented through a provocative and challenging approach – the question-and-answer method.

A climate of success is established by furnishing the correct answers at the end of each test.

You soon learn to recognize types of questions, forms of questions, and patterns of questioning. You may even begin to anticipate expected outcomes.

You perceive that many questions are repeated or adapted so that you can gain acute insights, which may enable you to score many sure points.

You learn how to confront new questions, or types of questions, and to attack them confidently and work out the correct answers.

You note objectives and emphases, and recognize pitfalls and dangers, so that you may make positive educational adjustments.

Moreover, you are kept fully informed in relation to new concepts, methods, practices, and directions in the field.

You discover that you are actually taking the examination all the time: you are preparing for the examination by "taking" an examination, not by reading extraneous and/or supererogatory textbooks.

In short, this PASSBOOK®, used directedly, should be an important factor in helping you to pass your test.

# WATER UTILITY WORKER

## DUTIES

Under general direction, performs semi-skilled and manual labor associated with the operation, construction, installation, replacement, cleaning, maintenance, and/or repair of the City's water, sewer collection and storm drain systems; and performs related duties as required.

Water Utility Worker I: This is the entry level class of this series in which employees perform a variety of semi-skilled and skilled duties in the construction, maintenance and operation of the City's water distribution, sewer collections and storm drain system infrastructures. Incumbents are generally hired at the Water Utility Worker I level and promoted to level II upon demonstrating competency and regularly performing the full range of duties within the division.

Water Utility Worker II: This is the journey level class of the series in which employees perform a full range of more complex assignments with minimal supervision. Installs, repairs and maintains the water distribution, sewer collection and storm drain systems (including retention ponds); operates and maintains pumping stations and camera equipment in the City's sewer collection system; services, maintains and repairs chlorination stations; operates and services equipment used in the repair, installation and maintenance of the systems including, but not limited to: compressors, jack hammers, backhoes, trenchers, tractors, and any other assigned light and heavy equipment; performs groundwater sampling; responds to customer calls; provides training and guidance in areas of specialization to unskilled workers; participates in after-hours emergency call-out duties; and performs other duties as assigned.

## KNOWLEDGE OF:

Both Classes: Basic concepts of equipment maintenance and repair; basic equipment and materials used in general construction work; uses of basic hand and power tools; basic safety considerations of maintenance work.

Water Utility Worker II: Equipment operation; techniques and methods used in the Water Utilities Division.

## SCOPE OF THE EXAMINATION

The examination will consist entirely of a written test comprised of multiple-choice questions, in which candidates may be examined for knowledge of: methods, materials, fittings, tools and equipment used in the installation, maintenance, and repair of water service, mains, water meters, and appurtenant materials; fittings, tools and equipment used in the installation, maintenance, and repair of water service mains, water meters, and appurtenant water distribution equipment; trenching and shoring practices; locating substructures; safety practices, including work area protection and traffic control; City personnel rules, policies and procedures; ability to: read water service maps, street guides, gate books, and construction prints; join pipe connections; tap water mains; use of power and hand tools weighing up to 90 lbs.; operate compressors, pumps and generators; deal tactfully and effectively with the public and crew members/co-workers; and other necessary skills, knowledge and abilities.

# HOW TO TAKE A TEST

I. YOU MUST PASS AN EXAMINATION

A. WHAT EVERY CANDIDATE SHOULD KNOW

Examination applicants often ask us for help in preparing for the written test. What can I study in advance? What kinds of questions will be asked? How will the test be given? How will the papers be graded?

As an applicant for a civil service examination, you may be wondering about some of these things. Our purpose here is to suggest effective methods of advance study and to describe civil service examinations.

Your chances for success on this examination can be increased if you know how to prepare. Those "pre-examination jitters" can be reduced if you know what to expect. You can even experience an adventure in good citizenship if you know why civil service exams are given.

B. WHY ARE CIVIL SERVICE EXAMINATIONS GIVEN?

Civil service examinations are important to you in two ways. As a citizen, you want public jobs filled by employees who know how to do their work. As a job seeker, you want a fair chance to compete for that job on an equal footing with other candidates. The best-known means of accomplishing this two-fold goal is the competitive examination.

Exams are widely publicized throughout the nation. They may be administered for jobs in federal, state, city, municipal, town or village governments or agencies.

Any citizen may apply, with some limitations, such as the age or residence of applicants. Your experience and education may be reviewed to see whether you meet the requirements for the particular examination. When these requirements exist, they are reasonable and applied consistently to all applicants. Thus, a competitive examination may cause you some uneasiness now, but it is your privilege and safeguard.

C. HOW ARE CIVIL SERVICE EXAMS DEVELOPED?

Examinations are carefully written by trained technicians who are specialists in the field known as "psychological measurement," in consultation with recognized authorities in the field of work that the test will cover. These experts recommend the subject matter areas or skills to be tested; only those knowledges or skills important to your success on the job are included. The most reliable books and source materials available are used as references. Together, the experts and technicians judge the difficulty level of the questions.

Test technicians know how to phrase questions so that the problem is clearly stated. Their ethics do not permit "trick" or "catch" questions. Questions may have been tried out on sample groups, or subjected to statistical analysis, to determine their usefulness.

Written tests are often used in combination with performance tests, ratings of training and experience, and oral interviews. All of these measures combine to form the best-known means of finding the right person for the right job.

## II. HOW TO PASS THE WRITTEN TEST

### A. NATURE OF THE EXAMINATION

To prepare intelligently for civil service examinations, you should know how they differ from school examinations you have taken. In school you were assigned certain definite pages to read or subjects to cover. The examination questions were quite detailed and usually emphasized memory. Civil service exams, on the other hand, try to discover your present ability to perform the duties of a position, plus your potentiality to learn these duties. In other words, a civil service exam attempts to predict how successful you will be. Questions cover such a broad area that they cannot be as minute and detailed as school exam questions.

In the public service similar kinds of work, or positions, are grouped together in one "class." This process is known as *position-classification*. All the positions in a class are paid according to the salary range for that class. One class title covers all of these positions, and they are all tested by the same examination.

### B. FOUR BASIC STEPS

#### 1) Study the announcement

How, then, can you know what subjects to study? Our best answer is: "Learn as much as possible about the class of positions for which you've applied." The exam will test the knowledge, skills and abilities needed to do the work.

Your most valuable source of information about the position you want is the official exam announcement. This announcement lists the training and experience qualifications. Check these standards and apply only if you come reasonably close to meeting them.

The brief description of the position in the examination announcement offers some clues to the subjects which will be tested. Think about the job itself. Review the duties in your mind. Can you perform them, or are there some in which you are rusty? Fill in the blank spots in your preparation.

Many jurisdictions preview the written test in the exam announcement by including a section called "Knowledge and Abilities Required," "Scope of the Examination," or some similar heading. Here you will find out specifically what fields will be tested.

#### 2) Review your own background

Once you learn in general what the position is all about, and what you need to know to do the work, ask yourself which subjects you already know fairly well and which need improvement. You may wonder whether to concentrate on improving your strong areas or on building some background in your fields of weakness. When the announcement has specified "some knowledge" or "considerable knowledge," or has used adjectives like "beginning principles of..." or "advanced ... methods," you can get a clue as to the number and difficulty of questions to be asked in any given field. More questions, and hence broader coverage, would be included for those subjects which are more important in the work. Now weigh your strengths and weaknesses against the job requirements and prepare accordingly.

#### 3) Determine the level of the position

Another way to tell how intensively you should prepare is to understand the level of the job for which you are applying. Is it the entering level? In other words, is this the position in which beginners in a field of work are hired? Or is it an intermediate or advanced level? Sometimes this is indicated by such words as "Junior" or "Senior" in the class title. Other jurisdictions use Roman numerals to designate the level – Clerk I, Clerk II, for example. The word "Supervisor" sometimes appears in the title. If the level is not indicated by the title, check the description of duties. Will you be working under very close supervision, or will you have responsibility for independent decisions in this work?

### 4) Choose appropriate study materials

Now that you know the subjects to be examined and the relative amount of each subject to be covered, you can choose suitable study materials. For beginning level jobs, or even advanced ones, if you have a pronounced weakness in some aspect of your training, read a modern, standard textbook in that field. Be sure it is up to date and has general coverage. Such books are normally available at your library, and the librarian will be glad to help you locate one. For entry-level positions, questions of appropriate difficulty are chosen -- neither highly advanced questions, nor those too simple. Such questions require careful thought but not advanced training.

If the position for which you are applying is technical or advanced, you will read more advanced, specialized material. If you are already familiar with the basic principles of your field, elementary textbooks would waste your time. Concentrate on advanced textbooks and technical periodicals. Think through the concepts and review difficult problems in your field.

These are all general sources. You can get more ideas on your own initiative, following these leads. For example, training manuals and publications of the government agency which employs workers in your field can be useful, particularly for technical and professional positions. A letter or visit to the government department involved may result in more specific study suggestions, and certainly will provide you with a more definite idea of the exact nature of the position you are seeking.

## III. KINDS OF TESTS

Tests are used for purposes other than measuring knowledge and ability to perform specified duties. For some positions, it is equally important to test ability to make adjustments to new situations or to profit from training. In others, basic mental abilities not dependent on information are essential. Questions which test these things may not appear as pertinent to the duties of the position as those which test for knowledge and information. Yet they are often highly important parts of a fair examination. For very general questions, it is almost impossible to help you direct your study efforts. What we can do is to point out some of the more common of these general abilities needed in public service positions and describe some typical questions.

1) General information

Broad, general information has been found useful for predicting job success in some kinds of work. This is tested in a variety of ways, from vocabulary lists to questions about current events. Basic background in some field of work, such as sociology or economics, may be sampled in a group of questions. Often these are principles which have become familiar to most persons through exposure rather than through formal training. It is difficult to advise you how to study for these questions; being alert to the world around you is our best suggestion.

2) Verbal ability

An example of an ability needed in many positions is verbal or language ability. Verbal ability is, in brief, the ability to use and understand words. Vocabulary and grammar tests are typical measures of this ability. Reading comprehension or paragraph interpretation questions are common in many kinds of civil service tests. You are given a paragraph of written material and asked to find its central meaning.

3) **Numerical ability**

Number skills can be tested by the familiar arithmetic problem, by checking paired lists of numbers to see which are alike and which are different, or by interpreting charts and graphs. In the latter test, a graph may be printed in the test booklet which you are asked to use as the basis for answering questions.

4) **Observation**

A popular test for law-enforcement positions is the observation test. A picture is shown to you for several minutes, then taken away. Questions about the picture test your ability to observe both details and larger elements.

5) **Following directions**

In many positions in the public service, the employee must be able to carry out written instructions dependably and accurately. You may be given a chart with several columns, each column listing a variety of information. The questions require you to carry out directions involving the information given in the chart.

6) **Skills and aptitudes**

Performance tests effectively measure some manual skills and aptitudes. When the skill is one in which you are trained, such as typing or shorthand, you can practice. These tests are often very much like those given in business school or high school courses. For many of the other skills and aptitudes, however, no short-time preparation can be made. Skills and abilities natural to you or that you have developed throughout your lifetime are being tested.

Many of the general questions just described provide all the data needed to answer the questions and ask you to use your reasoning ability to find the answers. Your best preparation for these tests, as well as for tests of facts and ideas, is to be at your physical and mental best. You, no doubt, have your own methods of getting into an exam-taking mood and keeping "in shape." The next section lists some ideas on this subject.

## IV. KINDS OF QUESTIONS

Only rarely is the "essay" question, which you answer in narrative form, used in civil service tests. Civil service tests are usually of the short-answer type. Full instructions for answering these questions will be given to you at the examination. But in case this is your first experience with short-answer questions and separate answer sheets, here is what you need to know:

1) **Multiple-choice Questions**

Most popular of the short-answer questions is the "multiple choice" or "best answer" question. It can be used, for example, to test for factual knowledge, ability to solve problems or judgment in meeting situations found at work.

A multiple-choice question is normally one of three types—
- It can begin with an incomplete statement followed by several possible endings. You are to find the one ending which *best* completes the statement, although some of the others may not be entirely wrong.
- It can also be a complete statement in the form of a question which is answered by choosing one of the statements listed.

- It can be in the form of a problem – again you select the best answer.

Here is an example of a multiple-choice question with a discussion which should give you some clues as to the method for choosing the right answer:

When an employee has a complaint about his assignment, the action which will *best* help him overcome his difficulty is to
- A. discuss his difficulty with his coworkers
- B. take the problem to the head of the organization
- C. take the problem to the person who gave him the assignment
- D. say nothing to anyone about his complaint

In answering this question, you should study each of the choices to find which is best. Consider choice "A" – Certainly an employee may discuss his complaint with fellow employees, but no change or improvement can result, and the complaint remains unresolved. Choice "B" is a poor choice since the head of the organization probably does not know what assignment you have been given, and taking your problem to him is known as "going over the head" of the supervisor. The supervisor, or person who made the assignment, is the person who can clarify it or correct any injustice. Choice "C" is, therefore, correct. To say nothing, as in choice "D," is unwise. Supervisors have and interest in knowing the problems employees are facing, and the employee is seeking a solution to his problem.

## 2) True/False Questions

The "true/false" or "right/wrong" form of question is sometimes used. Here a complete statement is given. Your job is to decide whether the statement is right or wrong.

SAMPLE: A roaming cell-phone call to a nearby city costs less than a non-roaming call to a distant city.

This statement is wrong, or false, since roaming calls are more expensive.

This is not a complete list of all possible question forms, although most of the others are variations of these common types. You will always get complete directions for answering questions. Be sure you understand *how* to mark your answers – ask questions until you do.

## V. RECORDING YOUR ANSWERS

Computer terminals are used more and more today for many different kinds of exams.
For an examination with very few applicants, you may be told to record your answers in the test booklet itself. Separate answer sheets are much more common. If this separate answer sheet is to be scored by machine – and this is often the case – it is highly important that you mark your answers correctly in order to get credit.

An electronic scoring machine is often used in civil service offices because of the speed with which papers can be scored. Machine-scored answer sheets must be marked with a pencil, which will be given to you. This pencil has a high graphite content which responds to the electronic scoring machine. As a matter of fact, stray dots may register as answers, so do not let your pencil rest on the answer sheet while you are pondering the correct answer. Also, if your pencil lead breaks or is otherwise defective, ask for another.

Since the answer sheet will be dropped in a slot in the scoring machine, be careful not to bend the corners or get the paper crumpled.

The answer sheet normally has five vertical columns of numbers, with 30 numbers to a column. These numbers correspond to the question numbers in your test booklet. After each number, going across the page are four or five pairs of dotted lines. These short dotted lines have small letters or numbers above them. The first two pairs may also have a "T" or "F" above the letters. This indicates that the first two pairs only are to be used if the questions are of the true-false type. If the questions are multiple choice, disregard the "T" and "F" and pay attention only to the small letters or numbers.

Answer your questions in the manner of the sample that follows:

32. The largest city in the United States is
    A. Washington, D.C.
    B. New York City
    C. Chicago
    D. Detroit
    E. San Francisco

1) Choose the answer you think is best. (New York City is the largest, so "B" is correct.)
2) Find the row of dotted lines numbered the same as the question you are answering. (Find row number 32)
3) Find the pair of dotted lines corresponding to the answer. (Find the pair of lines under the mark "B.")
4) Make a solid black mark between the dotted lines.


## VI. BEFORE THE TEST

Common sense will help you find procedures to follow to get ready for an examination. Too many of us, however, overlook these sensible measures. Indeed, nervousness and fatigue have been found to be the most serious reasons why applicants fail to do their best on civil service tests. Here is a list of reminders:

- Begin your preparation early – Don't wait until the last minute to go scurrying around for books and materials or to find out what the position is all about.
- Prepare continuously – An hour a night for a week is better than an all-night cram session. This has been definitely established. What is more, a night a week for a month will return better dividends than crowding your study into a shorter period of time.
- Locate the place of the exam – You have been sent a notice telling you when and where to report for the examination. If the location is in a different town or otherwise unfamiliar to you, it would be well to inquire the best route and learn something about the building.
- Relax the night before the test – Allow your mind to rest. Do not study at all that night. Plan some mild recreation or diversion; then go to bed early and get a good night's sleep.
- Get up early enough to make a leisurely trip to the place for the test – This way unforeseen events, traffic snarls, unfamiliar buildings, etc. will not upset you.
- Dress comfortably – A written test is not a fashion show. You will be known by number and not by name, so wear something comfortable.

- Leave excess paraphernalia at home – Shopping bags and odd bundles will get in your way. You need bring only the items mentioned in the official notice you received; usually everything you need is provided. Do not bring reference books to the exam. They will only confuse those last minutes and be taken away from you when in the test room.
- Arrive somewhat ahead of time – If because of transportation schedules you must get there very early, bring a newspaper or magazine to take your mind off yourself while waiting.
- Locate the examination room – When you have found the proper room, you will be directed to the seat or part of the room where you will sit. Sometimes you are given a sheet of instructions to read while you are waiting. Do not fill out any forms until you are told to do so; just read them and be prepared.
- Relax and prepare to listen to the instructions
- If you have any physical problem that may keep you from doing your best, be sure to tell the test administrator. If you are sick or in poor health, you really cannot do your best on the exam. You can come back and take the test some other time.

## VII. AT THE TEST

The day of the test is here and you have the test booklet in your hand. The temptation to get going is very strong. Caution! There is more to success than knowing the right answers. You must know how to identify your papers and understand variations in the type of short-answer question used in this particular examination. Follow these suggestions for maximum results from your efforts:

### 1) Cooperate with the monitor

The test administrator has a duty to create a situation in which you can be as much at ease as possible. He will give instructions, tell you when to begin, check to see that you are marking your answer sheet correctly, and so on. He is not there to guard you, although he will see that your competitors do not take unfair advantage. He wants to help you do your best.

### 2) Listen to all instructions

Don't jump the gun! Wait until you understand all directions. In most civil service tests you get more time than you need to answer the questions. So don't be in a hurry. Read each word of instructions until you clearly understand the meaning. Study the examples, listen to all announcements and follow directions. Ask questions if you do not understand what to do.

### 3) Identify your papers

Civil service exams are usually identified by number only. You will be assigned a number; you must not put your name on your test papers. Be sure to copy your number correctly. Since more than one exam may be given, copy your exact examination title.

### 4) Plan your time

Unless you are told that a test is a "speed" or "rate of work" test, speed itself is usually not important. Time enough to answer all the questions will be provided, but this does not mean that you have all day. An overall time limit has been set. Divide the total time (in minutes) by the number of questions to determine the approximate time you have for each question.

**5) Do not linger over difficult questions**

If you come across a difficult question, mark it with a paper clip (useful to have along) and come back to it when you have been through the booklet. One caution if you do this – be sure to skip a number on your answer sheet as well. Check often to be sure that you have not lost your place and that you are marking in the row numbered the same as the question you are answering.

**6) Read the questions**

Be sure you know what the question asks! Many capable people are unsuccessful because they failed to *read* the questions correctly.

**7) Answer all questions**

Unless you have been instructed that a penalty will be deducted for incorrect answers, it is better to guess than to omit a question.

**8) Speed tests**

It is often better NOT to guess on speed tests. It has been found that on timed tests people are tempted to spend the last few seconds before time is called in marking answers at random – without even reading them – in the hope of picking up a few extra points. To discourage this practice, the instructions may warn you that your score will be "corrected" for guessing. That is, a penalty will be applied. The incorrect answers will be deducted from the correct ones, or some other penalty formula will be used.

**9) Review your answers**

If you finish before time is called, go back to the questions you guessed or omitted to give them further thought. Review other answers if you have time.

**10) Return your test materials**

If you are ready to leave before others have finished or time is called, take ALL your materials to the monitor and leave quietly. Never take any test material with you. The monitor can discover whose papers are not complete, and taking a test booklet may be grounds for disqualification.

## VIII. EXAMINATION TECHNIQUES

1) Read the general instructions carefully. These are usually printed on the first page of the exam booklet. As a rule, these instructions refer to the timing of the examination; the fact that you should not start work until the signal and must stop work at a signal, etc. If there are any *special* instructions, such as a choice of questions to be answered, make sure that you note this instruction carefully.

2) When you are ready to start work on the examination, that is as soon as the signal has been given, read the instructions to each question booklet, underline any key words or phrases, such as *least, best, outline, describe* and the like. In this way you will tend to answer as requested rather than discover on reviewing your paper that you *listed without describing*, that you selected the *worst* choice rather than the *best* choice, etc.

3) If the examination is of the objective or multiple-choice type – that is, each question will also give a series of possible answers: A, B, C or D, and you are called upon to select the best answer and write the letter next to that answer on your answer paper – it is advisable to start answering each question in turn. There may be anywhere from 50 to 100 such questions in the three or four hours allotted and you can see how much time would be taken if you read through all the questions before beginning to answer any. Furthermore, if you come across a question or group of questions which you know would be difficult to answer, it would undoubtedly affect your handling of all the other questions.

4) If the examination is of the essay type and contains but a few questions, it is a moot point as to whether you should read all the questions before starting to answer any one. Of course, if you are given a choice – say five out of seven and the like – then it is essential to read all the questions so you can eliminate the two that are most difficult. If, however, you are asked to answer all the questions, there may be danger in trying to answer the easiest one first because you may find that you will spend too much time on it. The best technique is to answer the first question, then proceed to the second, etc.

5) Time your answers. Before the exam begins, write down the time it started, then add the time allowed for the examination and write down the time it must be completed, then divide the time available somewhat as follows:
   - If 3-1/2 hours are allowed, that would be 210 minutes. If you have 80 objective-type questions, that would be an average of 2-1/2 minutes per question. Allow yourself no more than 2 minutes per question, or a total of 160 minutes, which will permit about 50 minutes to review.
   - If for the time allotment of 210 minutes there are 7 essay questions to answer, that would average about 30 minutes a question. Give yourself only 25 minutes per question so that you have about 35 minutes to review.

6) The most important instruction is to *read each question* and make sure you know what is wanted. The second most important instruction is to *time yourself properly* so that you answer every question. The third most important instruction is to *answer every question*. Guess if you have to but include something for each question. Remember that you will receive no credit for a blank and will probably receive some credit if you write something in answer to an essay question. If you guess a letter – say "B" for a multiple-choice question – you may have guessed right. If you leave a blank as an answer to a multiple-choice question, the examiners may respect your feelings but it will not add a point to your score. Some exams may penalize you for wrong answers, so in such cases *only*, you may not want to guess unless you have some basis for your answer.

7) Suggestions
   a. Objective-type questions
      1. Examine the question booklet for proper sequence of pages and questions
      2. Read all instructions carefully
      3. Skip any question which seems too difficult; return to it after all other questions have been answered
      4. Apportion your time properly; do not spend too much time on any single question or group of questions

5. Note and underline key words – *all, most, fewest, least, best, worst, same, opposite,* etc.
6. Pay particular attention to negatives
7. Note unusual option, e.g., unduly long, short, complex, different or similar in content to the body of the question
8. Observe the use of "hedging" words – *probably, may, most likely,* etc.
9. Make sure that your answer is put next to the same number as the question
10. Do not second-guess unless you have good reason to believe the second answer is definitely more correct
11. Cross out original answer if you decide another answer is more accurate; do not erase until you are ready to hand your paper in
12. Answer all questions; guess unless instructed otherwise
13. Leave time for review

  b. Essay questions
1. Read each question carefully
2. Determine exactly what is wanted. Underline key words or phrases.
3. Decide on outline or paragraph answer
4. Include many different points and elements unless asked to develop any one or two points or elements
5. Show impartiality by giving pros and cons unless directed to select one side only
6. Make and write down any assumptions you find necessary to answer the questions
7. Watch your English, grammar, punctuation and choice of words
8. Time your answers; don't crowd material

8) Answering the essay question

Most essay questions can be answered by framing the specific response around several key words or ideas. Here are a few such key words or ideas:

M's: manpower, materials, methods, money, management
P's: purpose, program, policy, plan, procedure, practice, problems, pitfalls, personnel, public relations

  a. Six basic steps in handling problems:
1. Preliminary plan and background development
2. Collect information, data and facts
3. Analyze and interpret information, data and facts
4. Analyze and develop solutions as well as make recommendations
5. Prepare report and sell recommendations
6. Install recommendations and follow up effectiveness

  b. Pitfalls to avoid
1. *Taking things for granted* – A statement of the situation does not necessarily imply that each of the elements is necessarily true; for example, a complaint may be invalid and biased so that all that can be taken for granted is that a complaint has been registered

2. *Considering only one side of a situation* – Wherever possible, indicate several alternatives and then point out the reasons you selected the best one
3. *Failing to indicate follow up* – Whenever your answer indicates action on your part, make certain that you will take proper follow-up action to see how successful your recommendations, procedures or actions turn out to be
4. *Taking too long in answering any single question* – Remember to time your answers properly

## IX. AFTER THE TEST

Scoring procedures differ in detail among civil service jurisdictions although the general principles are the same. Whether the papers are hand-scored or graded by machine we have described, they are nearly always graded by number. That is, the person who marks the paper knows only the number – never the name – of the applicant. Not until all the papers have been graded will they be matched with names. If other tests, such as training and experience or oral interview ratings have been given, scores will be combined. Different parts of the examination usually have different weights. For example, the written test might count 60 percent of the final grade, and a rating of training and experience 40 percent. In many jurisdictions, veterans will have a certain number of points added to their grades.

After the final grade has been determined, the names are placed in grade order and an eligible list is established. There are various methods for resolving ties between those who get the same final grade – probably the most common is to place first the name of the person whose application was received first. Job offers are made from the eligible list in the order the names appear on it. You will be notified of your grade and your rank as soon as all these computations have been made. This will be done as rapidly as possible.

People who are found to meet the requirements in the announcement are called "eligibles." Their names are put on a list of eligible candidates. An eligible's chances of getting a job depend on how high he stands on this list and how fast agencies are filling jobs from the list.

When a job is to be filled from a list of eligibles, the agency asks for the names of people on the list of eligibles for that job. When the civil service commission receives this request, it sends to the agency the names of the three people highest on this list. Or, if the job to be filled has specialized requirements, the office sends the agency the names of the top three persons who meet these requirements from the general list.

The appointing officer makes a choice from among the three people whose names were sent to him. If the selected person accepts the appointment, the names of the others are put back on the list to be considered for future openings.

That is the rule in hiring from all kinds of eligible lists, whether they are for typist, carpenter, chemist, or something else. For every vacancy, the appointing officer has his choice of any one of the top three eligibles on the list. This explains why the person whose name is on top of the list sometimes does not get an appointment when some of the persons lower on the list do. If the appointing officer chooses the second or third eligible, the No. 1 eligible does not get a job at once, but stays on the list until he is appointed or the list is terminated.

# X. HOW TO PASS THE INTERVIEW TEST

The examination for which you applied requires an oral interview test. You have already taken the written test and you are now being called for the interview test – the final part of the formal examination.

You may think that it is not possible to prepare for an interview test and that there are no procedures to follow during an interview. Our purpose is to point out some things you can do in advance that will help you and some good rules to follow and pitfalls to avoid while you are being interviewed.

*What is an interview supposed to test?*

The written examination is designed to test the technical knowledge and competence of the candidate; the oral is designed to evaluate intangible qualities, not readily measured otherwise, and to establish a list showing the relative fitness of each candidate – as measured against his competitors – for the position sought. Scoring is not on the basis of "right" and "wrong," but on a sliding scale of values ranging from "not passable" to "outstanding." As a matter of fact, it is possible to achieve a relatively low score without a single "incorrect" answer because of evident weakness in the qualities being measured.

Occasionally, an examination may consist entirely of an oral test – either an individual or a group oral. In such cases, information is sought concerning the technical knowledges and abilities of the candidate, since there has been no written examination for this purpose. More commonly, however, an oral test is used to supplement a written examination.

*Who conducts interviews?*

The composition of oral boards varies among different jurisdictions. In nearly all, a representative of the personnel department serves as chairman. One of the members of the board may be a representative of the department in which the candidate would work. In some cases, "outside experts" are used, and, frequently, a businessman or some other representative of the general public is asked to serve. Labor and management or other special groups may be represented. The aim is to secure the services of experts in the appropriate field.

However the board is composed, it is a good idea (and not at all improper or unethical) to ascertain in advance of the interview who the members are and what groups they represent. When you are introduced to them, you will have some idea of their backgrounds and interests, and at least you will not stutter and stammer over their names.

*What should be done before the interview?*

While knowledge about the board members is useful and takes some of the surprise element out of the interview, there is other preparation which is more substantive. It *is* possible to prepare for an oral interview – in several ways:

**1) Keep a copy of your application and review it carefully before the interview**

This may be the only document before the oral board, and the starting point of the interview. Know what education and experience you have listed there, and the sequence and dates of all of it. Sometimes the board will ask you to review the highlights of your experience for them; you should not have to hem and haw doing it.

**2) Study the class specification and the examination announcement**

Usually, the oral board has one or both of these to guide them. The qualities, characteristics or knowledges required by the position sought are stated in these documents. They offer valuable clues as to the nature of the oral interview. For example, if the job involves supervisory responsibilities, the announcement will usually indicate that knowledge of modern supervisory methods and the qualifications of the candidate as a supervisor will be tested. If so, you can expect such questions, frequently in the form of a hypothetical situation which you are expected to solve. NEVER go into an oral without knowledge of the duties and responsibilities of the job you seek.

### 3) Think through each qualification required

Try to visualize the kind of questions you would ask if you were a board member. How well could you answer them? Try especially to appraise your own knowledge and background in each area, *measured against the job sought*, and identify any areas in which you are weak. Be critical and realistic – do not flatter yourself.

### 4) Do some general reading in areas in which you feel you may be weak

For example, if the job involves supervision and your past experience has NOT, some general reading in supervisory methods and practices, particularly in the field of human relations, might be useful. Do NOT study agency procedures or detailed manuals. The oral board will be testing your understanding and capacity, not your memory.

### 5) Get a good night's sleep and watch your general health and mental attitude

You will want a clear head at the interview. Take care of a cold or any other minor ailment, and of course, no hangovers.

*What should be done on the day of the interview?*

Now comes the day of the interview itself. Give yourself plenty of time to get there. Plan to arrive somewhat ahead of the scheduled time, particularly if your appointment is in the fore part of the day. If a previous candidate fails to appear, the board might be ready for you a bit early. By early afternoon an oral board is almost invariably behind schedule if there are many candidates, and you may have to wait. Take along a book or magazine to read, or your application to review, but leave any extraneous material in the waiting room when you go in for your interview. In any event, relax and compose yourself.

The matter of dress is important. The board is forming impressions about you – from your experience, your manners, your attitude, and your appearance. Give your personal appearance careful attention. Dress your best, but not your flashiest. Choose conservative, appropriate clothing, and be sure it is immaculate. This is a business interview, and your appearance should indicate that you regard it as such. Besides, being well groomed and properly dressed will help boost your confidence.

Sooner or later, someone will call your name and escort you into the interview room. *This is it.* From here on you are on your own. It is too late for any more preparation. But remember, you asked for this opportunity to prove your fitness, and you are here because your request was granted.

*What happens when you go in?*

The usual sequence of events will be as follows: The clerk (who is often the board stenographer) will introduce you to the chairman of the oral board, who will introduce you to the other members of the board. Acknowledge the introductions before you sit down. Do not be surprised if you find a microphone facing you or a stenotypist sitting by. Oral interviews are usually recorded in the event of an appeal or other review.

Usually the chairman of the board will open the interview by reviewing the highlights of your education and work experience from your application – primarily for the benefit of the other members of the board, as well as to get the material into the record. Do not interrupt or comment unless there is an error or significant misinterpretation; if that is the case, do not hesitate. But do not quibble about insignificant matters. Also, he will usually ask you some question about your education, experience or your present job – partly to get you to start talking and to establish the interviewing "rapport." He may start the actual questioning, or turn it over to one of the other members. Frequently, each member undertakes the questioning on a particular area, one in which he is perhaps most competent, so you can expect each member to participate in the examination. Because time is limited, you may also expect some rather abrupt switches in the direction the questioning takes, so do not be upset by it. Normally, a board member will not pursue a single line of questioning unless he discovers a particular strength or weakness.

After each member has participated, the chairman will usually ask whether any member has any further questions, then will ask you if you have anything you wish to add. Unless you are expecting this question, it may floor you. Worse, it may start you off on an extended, extemporaneous speech. The board is not usually seeking more information. The question is principally to offer you a last opportunity to present further qualifications or to indicate that you have nothing to add. So, if you feel that a significant qualification or characteristic has been overlooked, it is proper to point it out in a sentence or so. Do not compliment the board on the thoroughness of their examination – they have been sketchy, and you know it. If you wish, merely say, "No thank you, I have nothing further to add." This is a point where you can "talk yourself out" of a good impression or fail to present an important bit of information. Remember, *you close the interview yourself.*

The chairman will then say, "That is all, Mr. _____, thank you." Do not be startled; the interview is over, and quicker than you think. Thank him, gather your belongings and take your leave. Save your sigh of relief for the other side of the door.


*How to put your best foot forward*
Throughout this entire process, you may feel that the board individually and collectively is trying to pierce your defenses, seek out your hidden weaknesses and embarrass and confuse you. Actually, this is not true. They are obliged to make an appraisal of your qualifications for the job you are seeking, and they want to see you in your best light. Remember, they must interview all candidates and a non-cooperative candidate may become a failure in spite of their best efforts to bring out his qualifications. Here are 15 suggestions that will help you:

**1) Be natural – Keep your attitude confident, not cocky**
If you are not confident that you can do the job, do not expect the board to be. Do not apologize for your weaknesses, try to bring out your strong points. The board is interested in a positive, not negative, presentation. Cockiness will antagonize any board member and make him wonder if you are covering up a weakness by a false show of strength.

**2) Get comfortable, but don't lounge or sprawl**
Sit erectly but not stiffly. A careless posture may lead the board to conclude that you are careless in other things, or at least that you are not impressed by the importance of the occasion. Either conclusion is natural, even if incorrect. Do not fuss with your clothing, a pencil or an ashtray. Your hands may occasionally be useful to emphasize a point; do not let them become a point of distraction.

**3) Do not wisecrack or make small talk**
This is a serious situation, and your attitude should show that you consider it as such. Further, the time of the board is limited – they do not want to waste it, and neither should you.

**4) Do not exaggerate your experience or abilities**

In the first place, from information in the application or other interviews and sources, the board may know more about you than you think. Secondly, you probably will not get away with it. An experienced board is rather adept at spotting such a situation, so do not take the chance.

**5) If you know a board member, do not make a point of it, yet do not hide it**

Certainly you are not fooling him, and probably not the other members of the board. Do not try to take advantage of your acquaintanceship – it will probably do you little good.

**6) Do not dominate the interview**

Let the board do that. They will give you the clues – do not assume that you have to do all the talking. Realize that the board has a number of questions to ask you, and do not try to take up all the interview time by showing off your extensive knowledge of the answer to the first one.

**7) Be attentive**

You only have 20 minutes or so, and you should keep your attention at its sharpest throughout. When a member is addressing a problem or question to you, give him your undivided attention. Address your reply principally to him, but do not exclude the other board members.

**8) Do not interrupt**

A board member may be stating a problem for you to analyze. He will ask you a question when the time comes. Let him state the problem, and wait for the question.

**9) Make sure you understand the question**

Do not try to answer until you are sure what the question is. If it is not clear, restate it in your own words or ask the board member to clarify it for you. However, do not haggle about minor elements.

**10) Reply promptly but not hastily**

A common entry on oral board rating sheets is "candidate responded readily," or "candidate hesitated in replies." Respond as promptly and quickly as you can, but do not jump to a hasty, ill-considered answer.

**11) Do not be peremptory in your answers**

A brief answer is proper – but do not fire your answer back. That is a losing game from your point of view. The board member can probably ask questions much faster than you can answer them.

**12) Do not try to create the answer you think the board member wants**

He is interested in what kind of mind you have and how it works – not in playing games. Furthermore, he can usually spot this practice and will actually grade you down on it.

**13) Do not switch sides in your reply merely to agree with a board member**

Frequently, a member will take a contrary position merely to draw you out and to see if you are willing and able to defend your point of view. Do not start a debate, yet do not surrender a good position. If a position is worth taking, it is worth defending.

**14) Do not be afraid to admit an error in judgment if you are shown to be wrong**

The board knows that you are forced to reply without any opportunity for careful consideration. Your answer may be demonstrably wrong. If so, admit it and get on with the interview.

**15) Do not dwell at length on your present job**

The opening question may relate to your present assignment. Answer the question but do not go into an extended discussion. You are being examined for a *new* job, not your present one. As a matter of fact, try to phrase ALL your answers in terms of the job for which you are being examined.

*Basis of Rating*

Probably you will forget most of these "do's" and "don'ts" when you walk into the oral interview room. Even remembering them all will not ensure you a passing grade. Perhaps you did not have the qualifications in the first place. But remembering them will help you to put your best foot forward, without treading on the toes of the board members.

Rumor and popular opinion to the contrary notwithstanding, an oral board wants you to make the best appearance possible. They know you are under pressure – but they also want to see how you respond to it as a guide to what your reaction would be under the pressures of the job you seek. They will be influenced by the degree of poise you display, the personal traits you show and the manner in which you respond.


ABOUT THIS BOOK

This book contains tests divided into Examination Sections. Go through each test, answering every question in the margin. We have also attached a sample answer sheet at the back of the book that can be removed and used. At the end of each test look at the answer key and check your answers. On the ones you got wrong, look at the right answer choice and learn. Do not fill in the answers first. Do not memorize the questions and answers, but understand the answer and principles involved. On your test, the questions will likely be different from the samples. Questions are changed and new ones added. If you understand these past questions you should have success with any changes that arise. Tests may consist of several types of questions. We have additional books on each subject should more study be advisable or necessary for you. Finally, the more you study, the better prepared you will be. This book is intended to be the last thing you study before you walk into the examination room. Prior study of relevant texts is also recommended. NLC publishes some of these in our Fundamental Series. Knowledge and good sense are important factors in passing your exam. Good luck also helps. So now study this Passbook, absorb the material contained within and take that knowledge into the examination. Then do your best to pass that exam.

# EXAMINATION SECTION

# EXAMINATION SECTION
# TEST 1

DIRECTIONS: Each question or incomplete statement is followed by several suggested answers or completions. Select the one that BEST answers the question or completes the statement. *PRINT THE LETTER OF THE CORRECT ANSWER IN THE SPACE AT THE RIGHT.*

1. A Bourdon tube gage is used to measure  1.____

   A. temperature  B. acidity
   C. turbidity  D. pressure

2. An instrument used to locate buried metallic pipes is known as a(n)  2.____

   A. scleroscope  B. M-scope
   C. kinoscope  D. oscilloscope

3. The PRIMARY function of a check valve is to  3.____

   A. prevent the illegal use of fire hydrants
   B. insure adequate water pressure in high buildings
   C. prevent freezing of water
   D. permit flow of water in one direction only

4. Of the following, the torque applied by a ratchet wrench would be expressed in units of  4.____

   A. horsepower  B. pounds
   C. pounds per square inch  D. foot-pounds

5. Most lead joints runners are made of  5.____

   A. nylon  B. asbestos
   C. leadite  D. polyethylene

6. The tool shown in the sketch at the right is a  6.____

   A. pickout iron
   B. pipe jointer
   C. cover bolt wrench
   D. pipe reamer

7. In order to reduce the force necessary to open or close large gate valves, the valves are equipped with a  7.____

   A. vacuum breaker  B. by-pass
   C. saddle  D. shear gate

8. In order to open a ground-key valve, used as a corporation cock to full flow, it is necessary to rotate the handle _____ degrees.  8.____

   A. 45  B. 60  C. 75  D. 90

1

9. A foot valve is MOST often used

   A. to relieve excess pressure in a water main
   B. on the suction pipe of a centrifugal pump
   C. at the high point in a pipeline
   D. to drain a pipeline

10. Of the following tools, the one that generally should NOT be used to tighten screwed piping is a _____ wrench.

    A. Stillson          B. strap
    C. monkey            D. chain

11. A 6-inch branch may be connected to an 8-inch main without shutting off the flow of water by using a

    A. tapping valve and sleeve
    B. cutting in tee
    C. cutting in valve and sleeve
    D. pipe tong

12. When water flows through a thirty-second bend, the direction of flow changes

    A. 11 1/4°     B. 22 1/2°     C. 45°     D. 90°

13. A main in which water is flowing east is connected to a pipe offset. As the water leaves the offset, it will be flowing toward the

    A. north       B. south       C. east    D. west

14. An electrolysis test connection on a water main is used to measure the

    A. salinity of the ground water outside the main
    B. the chlorine residual in the water in the main
    C. stray electric current in the main
    D. temperature of the ground around the main

15. A common method of temporarily lowering the ground water below the level of operations in a trench is by the use of

    A. wellpoints        B. mud valves
    C. piles             D. trenching machines

16. The diameter of a #6 steel reinforcing bar is MOST NEARLY

    A. 1"          B. 3/4"        C. 1/2"    D. 1/4"

17. The quick opening or closing of valves or gates, and the sudden starting, stopping, or variation in speed of pumps is FREQUENTLY the cause of

    A. sluggish flow of water    B. water-borne diseases
    C. water hammer              D. water hardness

18. Poured lead pipe joints must be calked MAINLY because the hot lead

    A. corrodes some of the cast iron    B. burns some of the jute
    C. becomes porous on cooling         D. shrinks on cooling

19. Flexibility between a water main and a service pipe can be obtained by the use of a

    A. corporation cock
    B. gooseneck
    C. curb stop
    D. air-release valve

20. It is necessary to shut off the water in a main temporarily in order to make repairs. In order to get cooperation from the general public, the

    A. job should be done at night so that few people will be aware of it
    B. shut-off crew should be ordered not to speak to the general public
    C. job should be done in several stages so that the public realizes how difficult the problem is
    D. purpose and duration of the shut-off should be explained to the general public

Questions 21-25.

DIRECTIONS: Questions 21 through 25 are to be answered on the basis of maps or diagrams used by departments of water resources.

21. On a distribution map, the symbol ———— — ———— refers to a main whose diameter is

    A. 6"
    B. 8"
    C. 10"
    D. 12"

22. On a distribution map, the symbol ⚲ refers to a

    A. gate valve
    B. blow-off
    C. air-cock
    D. regulator

23. On a distribution map, the symbol ——+—— refers to a

    A. gate valve
    B. 3-way
    C. 4-way
    D. reducer

24. On a distribution map, the symbol ↓ refers to a

    A. hydrant
    B. air-cock
    C. 3-way
    D. 4-way

25. On a work area diagram, the symbol ▨ refers to a(n)

    A. office
    B. truck
    C. barricade
    D. excavation.

## KEY (CORRECT ANSWERS)

| | | | |
|---|---|---|---|
| 1. | D | 11. | A |
| 2. | B | 12. | A |
| 3. | D | 13. | C |
| 4. | D | 14. | C |
| 5. | B | 15. | A |
| 6. | D | 16. | B |
| 7. | B | 17. | C |
| 8. | D | 18. | D |
| 9. | B | 19. | B |
| 10. | C | 20. | D |

21. B
22. B
23. A
24. C
25. D

# TEST 2

DIRECTIONS: Each question or incomplete statement is followed by several suggested answers or completions. Select the one that BEST answers the question or completes the statement. *PRINT THE LETTER OF THE CORRECT ANSWER IN THE SPACE AT THE RIGHT.*

1. According to standard water main specifications, prior to laying any straight pipe or special castings, the inside surfaces shall be mopped or sprayed with a chlorine solution containing not less than 150 _____ of chlorine.

    A. quarts  B. lbs.  C. p.p.m.  D. tanks

    1._____

2. When water main repairs are underway on the north side of a two-way street which runs east and west, the location recommended by the Department of Water Resources of a lead heating burner is _____ of the excavation.

    A. north  B. east  C. south  D. west

    2._____

3. Of the following statements, the one which is NOT included on the official water supply shut-off notice is

    A. turn off water-cooled refrigerating and air conditioning units
    B. close main house valve on water pipe supplying premises
    C. drain all water pipes above the basement
    D. open, as a vent, one hot water faucet above the level of the hot water storage tank

    3._____

4. In order to obtain a Temporary Street Opening Permit, the applicant must be a

    A. city resident            B. city employee
    C. licensed plumber         D. professional engineer

    4._____

5. In accordance with standard water main specifications, all water mains 20 inches in diameter or larger shall be subjected to a leakage test at a pressure of 125 psi. The leakage shall NOT be greater than

    A. twenty gallons per 24 hours
    B. two gallons per linear foot of pipe joint per 24 hours
    C. two gallons per linear foot of pipe joint per 20 minutes
    D. twenty gallons per mile of pipe per 24 hours

    5._____

6. In accordance with official specifications, in paved streets the length of trench that may be opened between the point where the backfilling has been completed and the point where the pavement is being removed shall NOT exceed

    A. the width of the street
    B. fifteen hundred feet for pipes 24 inches or less in diameter
    C. five hundred feet for all pipe diameters
    D. the distance between hydrants

    6._____

Questions 7-10.

DIRECTIONS: Questions 7 through 10 are to be answered SOLELY on the basis of the following passage.

5

The choice of equipment to be used in excavating a trench will depend on the job conditions, the depth and width of the trench, the class of the soil, the extent to which ground water is present, the width of the right of way for the disposal of excavated earth, and the type of equipment already owned by a contractor.

If a relatively shallow and narrow trench is to be excavated in firm soil, the wheel-type trenching machine is probably the most suitable. However, if the soil is rock, which requires blasting, the most suitable excavator will be a hoe, or a less desirable substitute could be a dragline. If the soil is unstable, water-saturated material, it may be necessary to use a dragline, hoe, or clamshell and let the walls establish a stable slope. If it is necessary to install solid sheeting to hold the walls in place, neither a hoe nor a dragline will work satisfactorily. A clamshell, which can excavate between the trench braces that hold the sheeting in place, probably will be the best equipment for the job.

7. According to the above passage, the wheel-type trenching machine is probably the MOST suitable for excavating

   A. unstable, water-saturated material
   B. when it is necessary to install solid sheeting
   C. a relatively shallow and narrow trench in firm soil
   D. when ground water is present

8. According to the above passage, the width of the right of way for the disposal of excavated earth

   A. depends upon the width of the street
   B. affects the depth of cover
   C. affects the choice of equipment to be used in excavating
   D. should be minimized to avoid inconveniencing the public

9. According to the above passage, a hoe will be the MOST suitable excavator if the

   A. soil is rock which requires blasting
   B. equipment is already owned by a contractor
   C. trench requires solid sheeting
   D. trench is over twenty feet deep

10. According to the above passage, the BEST equipment to use for excavating when it is necessary to install solid sheeting to hold the walls in place probably will be a

    A. clamshell
    B. dragline
    C. hoe
    D. wheel-type trenching machine

Questions 11-12.

DIRECTIONS: Questions 11 and 12 are to be answered SOLELY on the basis of the following passage.

Construction pumps frequently are required to perform under severe conditions, such as resulting from variations in the pumping head or from handling water that is muddy, sandy and trashy, or highly corrosive. The rate of pumping may vary several hundred percent during the period of construction. The most satisfactory solution to the pumping problem may be a single all-purpose pump, or it may be to use several types and sizes of pumps, to permit flexibility in the operations. The proper solution is to select the equipment which will take care of the pumping needs adequately at the lowest total cost.

11. According to the above passage, the PROPER solution to a construction pumping problem is to select equipment that has the lowest total cost which will also    11.____

    A. perform under severe conditions
    B. take care of the pumping needs adequately
    C. permit flexibility in operations
    D. provide maximum safety

12. According to the above passage, a variation of several hundred percent during the period of construction may occur in the    12.____

    A. pumping head
    B. rate of pumping
    C. volume of sandy and trashy water
    D. volume of highly corrosive water

Questions 13-14.

DIRECTIONS: Questions 13 and 14 are to be answered SOLELY on the basis of the following passage.

The mechanical failure of equipment may be the cause of a serious accident. Competent maintenance of equipment will reduce mechanical failures and in so doing reduce injuries and construction interruptions. Regular inspection of equipment will reduce maintenance expense.

13. Of the following, the BEST title for the above passage is    13.____

    A. Construction Productivity
    B. Preventive Maintenance of Equipment
    C. Inspection of Equipment
    D. Economical Construction

14. According to the above passage, the way to save money in construction work is to    14.____

    A. have qualified people operate equipment
    B. have periodic inspection of equipment
    C. have regular overhaul of equipment
    D. start a maintenance training program

15. Of the following items, the one MOST suitable for measuring the flow of water in a pipe is a    15.____

    A. poppet
    B. hydraulic ram
    C. cistern
    D. pitometer

16.

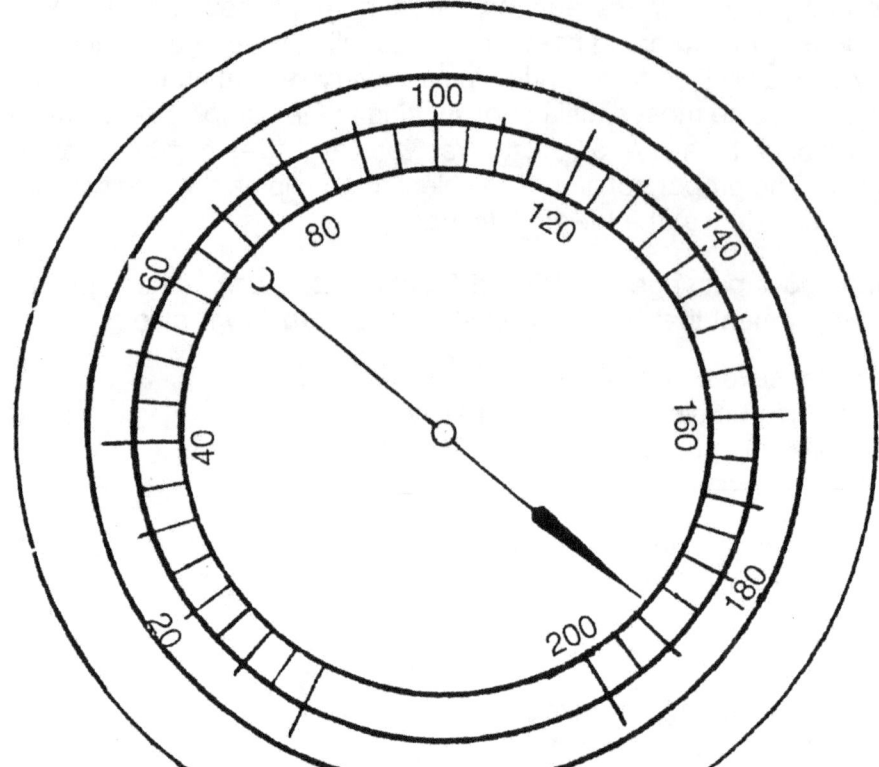

BOURDON DIAL

The reading indicated on the above dial is MOST NEARLY

A. 183 B. 188 C. 192 D. 196

17. An instrument used for detecting the sound of flowing water in a pipe network is a(n)

A. micrometer B. spectrometer
C. aquaphone D. viscophone

18. Of the following, the MAIN purpose of a Venturi meter is to measure the _____ in a main.

A. quantity of water flowing
B. chlorine content of the water
C. velocity of the water
D. temperature of the water

19. A blade with a small hole in the tip, used for measuring the flow from a hydrant, is a

A. hydrant pitot B. Venturi meter
C. parshall flume D. hydrant head

20. Hydrant-flow tests include observation of the pressure at a centrally situated hydrant and measurement of

   A. pressure at a group of neighboring hydrants
   B. flow from outlets at the top floor of a building
   C. reservoir elevation
   D. flow from a group of neighboring hydrants

21. Of the following, the one which is NOT a requirement of a satisfactory report is that it should be

   A. timely   B. lengthy   C. legible   D. accurate

22. When an accident occurs, the FIRST concern of the Foreman should be to

   A. see that injured person is properly cared for
   B. make sketches of the area
   C. interview the injured person
   D. interview witnesses and coworkers

23. Workers whose characteristics and behavior are such as to make them considerably more liable to injury than the average person are considered to be

   A. late
   C. careful
   B. safety conscious
   D. accident-prone

24. Safety inspections are not useful in an accident prevention program unless

   A. all persons who have accidents are fined
   B. insurance rates are decreased
   C. immediate action is taken to correct the conditions revealed
   D. there is adequate compensation for all injured parties

25. A Foreman is BEST qualified to investigate accidents involving his subordinates because he

   A. has all safety equipment for the job
   B. has more free time than his superiors
   C. has more skill than his superiors
   D. is familiar with all the job conditions

## KEY (CORRECT ANSWERS)

1. C
2. D
3. C
4. C
5. B
6. B
7. C
8. C
9. A
10. A

11. B
12. B
13. B
14. B
15. D
16. B
17. C
18. A
19. A
20. D

21. B
22. A
23. D
24. C
25. D

———

# EXAMINATION SECTION
## TEST 1

DIRECTIONS: Each question or incomplete statement is followed by several suggested answers or completions. Select the one that BEST answers the question or completes the statement. *PRINT THE LETTER OF THE CORRECT ANSWER IN THE SPACE AT THE RIGHT.*

Questions 1-5.

DIRECTIONS: Questions 1 through 5, inclusive, refer to the distribution map shown on the LAST page of this test. All questions are to be answered in accordance with this map.

1. The symbol just west of the boundary gate symbol on 21st Street between Willow Avenue and Meadow Avenue is a

   A. hydrant
   B. gate valve
   C. check valve
   D. reducer

2. The number of hydrants on the 30" main in Meadow Avenue between 22nd Street and 23rd Street is

   A. none   B. 1   C. 2   D. 3

3. The S symbol on the main at the west end of 18th Street means that the main is

   A. a special casting
   B. made of steel
   C. shut down
   D. high pressure service

4. A cap is located at or near the intersection of _____ Street and _____ Avenue.

   A. 24th; Willow
   B. 22nd; Willow
   C. 26th; Meadow
   D. 21st; Central

5. A blow off is located in

   A. Meadow Avenue between 19th & 20th Streets
   B. 22nd Street between Willow Avenue and Meadow Avenue
   C. Wilen Avenue between 22nd and 23rd Streets
   D. 22nd Street between Willow Avenue and Central Avenue

6. Assume that a normally sober man appears on the job intoxicated. Of the following, the BEST procedure for a foreman to follow is to

   A. give the man an easy job so that he cannot get hurt
   B. let the man *sleep it off* in the morning and put him to work in the afternoon
   C. let the man work at his normal duties but keep an *eye* on him
   D. send him home for the day

7. The Chief Engineer has decided to change the procedure that must be followed in making certain types of repairs. The one of the following statements concerning the new procedure that is CORRECT is:
   The men

A. should know why the procedure is being changed because they will then be more interested in the job
B. do not have to know the reason for the change because they need do only the work as they are told
C. should know why the procedure is being changed so that they can decide which method of doing the job is better
D. do not have to know the reason for the change because they are not capable of judging the best method of doing a job

8. A foreman, by mistake, orders his men to do a job improperly.  8_____
   Of the following, the BEST thing for the foreman to do when he realizes his error is to

   A. insist that the job be done as he ordered so that his mistake will not be discovered
   B. admit that he made the mistake and correct the order
   C. tell the men that the order came from *higher up so* that he will not be blamed for the mistake
   D. tell the men that he is merely trying this out to see if it works better

9. The BEST foreman is usually the  9_____

   A. fastest worker
   B. man who is most familiar with the streets in the borough
   C. strongest man
   D. man who is most tactful

10. A good foreman will  10_____

    A. look after the welfare of his men
    B. demand perfection in the work of his men at all times
    C. make special efforts to impress his superiors
    D. cover up for the actions of his men

11. As a newly appointed foreman, it is MOST important that you  11_____

    A. show the men who is boss by issuing orders
    B. prove to the men that you know more than they do
    C. become acquainted with the men and their abilities
    D. show the men how friendly you are

12. A foreman who criticizes his department head is a  12_____

    A. *good* foreman, because the men will feel he is on their side
    B. *poor* foreman, because the men will lose respect for him
    C. *good* foreman, because he will get more work done
    D. *poor* foreman, because he will have no time to do his own work

13. One of the men in your gang comes to you, the foreman, and complains that the men in  13_____
    the gang have taken a dislike to him and are making trouble for him.
    Of the following, the BEST thing for you to do is to

    A. tell the man he must learn to get along with the other men
    B. report the matter to your superior
    C. call the gang together and tell them they must stop making trouble
    D. investigate the complaint to determine what the problem is

14. As a foreman, you are inspecting the damage done by water from a broken main leaking into the basement of a store. After inspecting the damage, the owner complains to you about the conduct of the men who made the repair.
Of the following, the BEST way of handling this situation is to tell the owner that

    A. you are there to inspect the damage to the premises only
    B. he should make his complaint to higher authorities
    C. his complaint will be investigated and, if found correct, proper action will be taken
    D. nothing can be done at this time since the men are no longer at this location

14_____

Questions 15-17.

DIRECTIONS: Questions 15 through 17, inclusive, are based on the paragraph below. These questions are to be answered in accordance with the information given in this paragraph.

    Excavation of trench. The trench shall be excavated as directed; one side of the street or avenue shall be left open for traffic at all times. In paved streets, the length of trench that may be opened between the point where the backfilling has been completed and the point where the pavement is being removed shall not exceed fifteen hundred feet for pipes 24 inches or less in diameter. For pipes larger than 24 inch, the length of open trenches shall not exceed one thousand feet. The completion of the backfilling shall be interpreted to mean the backfilling of the trench and the consolidation of the backfill so that vehicular traffic can be resumed over the backfill, and also the placing of any temporary pavement that *may* be required.

15. According to the above paragraph, the street

    A. can be closed to traffic in emergencies
    B. can be closed to traffic only when laying more than 1500 feet of pipe
    C. is closed to traffic as directed
    D. shall be left open for traffic at all times

15_____

16. According to the above paragraph, the MAXIMUM length of open trench permitted in paved streets depends on the

    A. traffic on the street
    B. type of ground that is being excaVated
    C. water conditions met with in excavation
    D. diameter of the pipe being laid

16_____

17. According to the above paragraph, the one of the following items that is included in the *completion of the back-filling* is

    A. sheeting and bracing        B. cradle
    C. temporary pavement      D. bridging

17_____

Questions 18-20.

DIRECTIONS: Questions 18 through 20, inclusive, are based on the paragraph below. These questions are to be answered in accordance with the information given in this paragraph.

The Contractor shall notify the Engineer by noon of the day immediately preceding the date when he wishes to shut down any main, and if the time set be approved, the Contractor shall provide the men necessary to shut down the main at the time stipulated, and to previously notify all consumers whose supply may be affected. These men shall be under the direction of the Department employees, who will superintend all operations of valves and hydrants. Shutdowns for making connections will not be made unless and until the Contractor has everything on the ground in readiness for the work.

18. According to the above paragraph, before a contractor can make a shut-down, he MUST notify the

    A. Police Department
    B. district foreman
    C. engineer
    D. highway department

19. According to the above paragraph, the operation of the valves will be supervised by the

    A. department employees
    B. contractor's men
    C. contractor's superintendent
    D. engineer

20. According to the above paragraph, shut-downs for connections are made

    A. the day before the connection is made
    B. first and then consumers are notified
    C. at any time convenient to the contractor
    D. when the contractor has everything on the ground in readiness for the work

21. Water hammer in a pipe line is MOST frequently caused by _____ a valve too _____ .

    A. opening; rapidly
    B. opening; slowly
    C. closing; rapidly
    D. closing; slowly

22. In using a hacksaw, pressure should be applied to the hacksaw when

    A. pushing it
    B. pulling it
    C. pushing and pulling it
    D. either pushing or pulling, depending upon the way the cut is to be made

23. When cutting cast iron (other than pipe) with a hacksaw, the PROPER number of teeth per inch in the blade should be

    A. 14      B. 18      C. 24      D. 32

24. Concrete is a mixture of cement and

    A. lime, sand, and water
    B. sand and water
    C. sand and broken stone
    D. sand, broken stone, and water

25. The head of a cold chisel has mushroomed after considerable use.
The BEST thing to do is

   A. continue to use it since mushrooming is normal
   B. throw it away
   C. send it to the shop for redressing
   D. use a file to restore the head to its original shape

26. A valve box cover has been covered with asphalt during a street repaving job.
The BEST way to locate the valve is to use a

   A. geophone
   B. aquaphone
   C. distribution map and a tape
   D. probing bar

27. The number of cubic yards in a bin 4 feet by 8 feet by 13 feet is MOST NEARLY _____ cubic yards.

   A. 17  B. 15  C. 13  D. 11

28. The letter *P* stencilled on the roadside face of a hydrant indicates that the hydrant

   A. is a low pressure hydrant
   B. is a high pressure hydrant
   C. is out of service permanently
   D. has a plugged drain

29. A hydrant extension piece would MOST likely be used if

   A. the hydrant had been damaged
   B. an open trench exists in the street in front of the hydrant
   C. several hose lines must be connected to the hydrant
   D. the hose connections do not fit the hydrant nozzles

30. The drip valve of a hydrant

   A. should not open until after the hydrant valve has closed
   B. should open just before the hydrant valve has closed
   C. operates completely independent of the operation of the hydrant valve
   D. should only be closed during repair of the hydrant

31. To remove and replace the operating parts of a hydrant which is in service,

   A. the standpipe must be disconnected from the elbow
   B. it is necessary to do some excavating
   C. the main must be shut down
   D. no excavation is necessary

32. The material generally used for packing hydrant stems is

   A. asbestos         B. rubber cloth
   C. flax             D. leather

33. A roundabout would normally have as a component part a

   A. four-way   B. valve   C. plug   D. cap

34. Cast iron reducers are usually made in all but one of the following ways. The way in which they are NOT made is

   A. spigots on both ends
   B. hub on large end, spigot on small end
   C. hub on small end, spigot on large end
   D. hubs on both ends

35. A cast iron main running due east is to turn so that it runs N45W, that is, halfway between north and west. The change in direction could be made using _____ bends.

   A. sixteen 1/48   B. six 1/16
   C. four 1/8       D. two 1/4

36. A cast iron offset would NORMALLY be used

   A. to change the direction of a main
   B. when the main must run diagonally from one side of the street to the other
   C. when the main must be shifted parallel to itself several feet to avoid an existing structure
   D. when the main must be shifted several inches to avoid an existing structure

37. A 30-inch cast iron main is to be laid with a blow-off and an air cock. The cast iron piece used for the blow-off differs from that used for the air cock in

   A. size of outlet
   B. general shape
   C. material used
   D. length measured along the main

38. The upper part of a standard hydrant valve box is USUALLY connected to the lower part by

   A. screw threads       B. bolts
   C. a beaded rim        D. lugs and rods

39. A trench for an 18-inch cast iron main is being excavated in rock. The width of the trench should be AT LEAST _____ inches.

   A. 30   B. 36   C. 42   D. 48

40. Specifications of the Department of Water Supply, Gas and Electricity state that in a trench excavated in rock, projections of rock must be removed if they come within a certain distance of the outside of any portion of the pipe barrel or bell. This distance is, in inches,

   A. 4   B. 6   C. 8   D. 10

## KEY (CORRECT ANSWERS)

| | | | |
|---|---|---|---|
| 1. D | 11. C | 21. C | 31. D |
| 2. A | 12. B | 22. A | 32. C |
| 3. B | 13. D | 23. B | 33. B |
| 4. D | 14. C | 24. D | 34. D |
| 5. D | 15. D | 25. C | 35. B |
| 6. D | 16. D | 26. C | 36. D |
| 7. A | 17. C | 27. B | 37. A |
| 8. B | 18. C | 28. D | 38. A |
| 9. D | 19. A | 29. B | 39. C |
| 10. A | 20. D | 30. A | 40. B |

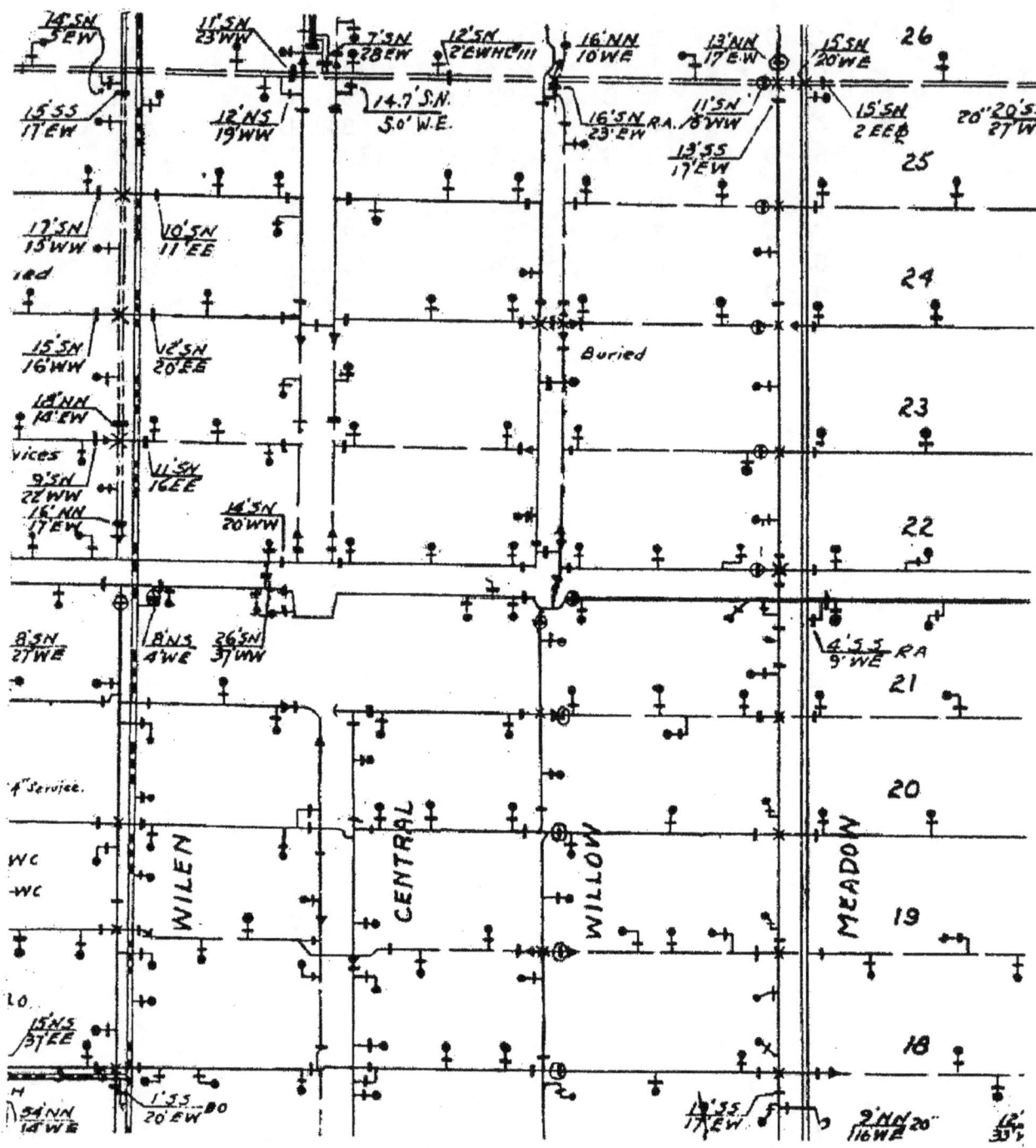

# TEST 2

DIRECTIONS: Each question or incomplete statement is followed by several suggested answers or completions. Select the one that BEST answers the question or completes the statement. *PRINT THE LETTER OF THE CORRECT ANSWER IN THE SPACE AT THE RIGHT.*

1. The MAXIMUM size of stones permitted in backfill is _____ inches.

   A. 12     B. 8     C. 4     D. 2

2. A two-inch galvanized steel pipe is to be connected to a cast iron main.
   The connection should be made by a standard corporation tap of the following size: _____ inch.

   A. 1     B. 1 1/2     C. 2     D. 2 1/2

3. Standard cast iron pipe of inside diameter from 12 to 20 inches may be furnished in nominal laying lengths up to and including _____ feet.

   A. 14     B. 16     C. 18     D. 20

4. The interior surface of new 12-inch cast iron pipe is USUALLY coated with

   A. cement mortar     B. nothing
   C. asphalt paint     D. coal tar pitch

5. A tarpaulin would MOST likely be used when

   A. mixing concrete
   B. running lead joints
   C. lowering pipe into a trench
   D. excavating a trench for a water main

6. Bands and bolts would be LEAST likely to be required at

   A. bends     B. branches     C. plugs     D. four-ways

7. A house service with a 3/8-inch tap on an existing main is to be transferred to a new main.
   The size of the tap on the new main should be _____ inch.

   A. 5/8     B. 1/2     C. 3/8     D. 1/4

8. The LARGEST tap permitted on a new 12-inch main is _____ inch.

   A. 1     B. 1 1/2     C. 2     D. 2 1/2

9. The sheeting of a trench serves

   A. only to protect workmen
   B. only to prevent damage to existing mains close to the trench
   C. only to prevent damage to pavement
   D. all three of the foregoing purposes

10. Water required for flushing backfill is USUALLY supplied

    A. in a fine spray
    B. by an ordinary garden hose
    C. from a tank truck
    D. through a flushing pipe

11. Water mains are USUALLY laid parallel to the curb at a distance of APPROXIMATELY _____ feet.

    A. 15    B. 12    C. 9    D. 6

12. After a main has been laid but prior to putting it into service, it should be disinfected by

    A. continuous flushing with water containing chlorine
    B. continuous flushing with clean water only
    C. introducing chlorine into the water in the pipe and letting the solution stand for 30 minutes
    D. blowing chlorine gas through the main

13. Before trimming a caulked pipe joint, the lead of a lead joint should

    A. extend outside the face of the bell
    B. be flush with the face of the bell
    C. be inside the face of the bell
    D. be heated

14. Drainage of hydrants require the use of lead lined pipe

    A. except when a cast iron drain base is provided
    B. except when the hydrant is connected to a sewer
    C. except when a blind drain is provided
    D. in every case

15. A standard cast iron reducer is to connect a 24-inch main to a smaller main. The length of the reducer USUALLY

    A. is the same regardless of the size of the smaller main
    B. decreases as the size of the smaller main decreases
    C. increases as the size of the smaller main decreases
    D. can be varied to fit the field conditions

16. A standard cast iron three-way does NOT have more than the following number of hubs:

    A. 3    B. 2    C. 1    D. 0

17. Of the following statements, the one which is CORRECT is:

    A. A cap is used on the spigot end of a pipe
    B. A plug is used on the spigot end of a pipe
    C. Caps and plugs can be used interchangeably
    D. Caps are usually available in larger sizes than plugs

18. Of the following statements, the one which is CORRECT is:

    A. A planned shutdown is not made rapidly
    B. In the event of an emergency shutdown, all valves in the area should be closed and then a study of the distribution map should be made to determine which valves can be opened
    C. Boundary gates should always be kept closed for the duration of an emergency shutdown
    D. The operation of all valves to be used in a planned shutdown should be checked prior to making the shutdown

19. When building material is stored on the street for the construction of a building,

    A. the Department of Water Supply, Gas and Electricity is not concerned
    B. there can be no objections if hydrants are accessible
    C. there can be no objections if the storage period is short
    D. serious difficulties for the Department of Water Supply, Gas and Electricity could result

20. A large steel main is to be emptied through a blow-off. The BEST way to proceed is to open

    A. the blow-off
    B. an aircock or hydrant at the high point of the main before opening the blow-off
    C. the blow-off and then open an air cock or hydrant at the high point of the main
    D. an air cock or hydrant at the low point of the main before opening the blow-off

21. A large new main is to be placed in service.
    To fill the main, it is important to FIRST open

    A. the head gate valve
    B. an air cock or hydrant on the main
    C. all side gate valves
    D. the side gate valves on one side of the main only

22. Of the following special castings, the one which is MOST like a blow-off is a

    A. four-way    B. reducer    C. three-way    D. offset

23. The laying length of a double hub

    A. is less than one foot
    B. depends upon the diameter of the pipe
    C. must be at least nine feet
    D. may be any length up to 20 feet, the maximum length depending upon the diameter

24. The gooseneck that is GENERALLY used to connect a service pipe to a main

    A. should be straight for its entire length
    B. comes in a standard length and, therefore, must be curved to make it fit

C. is deliberately curved so that it can accommodate movement between main and service pipe
D. is curved to provide extra length so that it can be cut and still be long enough to reconnect to the main

25. A non-rising stem gate valve would MOST likely be used when

   A. the threads of the stem must be readily accessible for lubrication
   B. space is limited
   C. the valve is used infrequently
   D. the valve is in a deep valve vault

26. Of the following types of valves, the one which is NOT usually found on water mains is the _____ valve.

   A. glove
   B. air relief
   C. pressure regulating
   D. gate

27. When a length of cast iron pipe is too long, it is USUALLY cut with a(n)

   A. chisel
   B. hacksaw
   C. emery wheel
   D. cutting torch

28. The PRINCIPAL objection to laying mains between December 15 and March 15 is with the

   A. freezing of water
   B. working conditions for the men
   C. freezing of soil
   D. the reduced length of daylight

29. A trench for a cast iron main is USUALLY backfilled immediately

   A. after the joints are caulked
   B. after the pressure test has been completed
   C. before water is placed in the main
   D. after water is placed in the main

30. When the pavement along the sides of a trench becomes undermined, the BEST thing to do is

   A. carefully tamp the backfill under the undermined pavement
   B. place a layer of broken stone on top of the backfill under the undermined pavement
   C. break down the undermined pavement before backfilling
   D. consolidate the backfill by thorough flushing

31. A small leak in a main would usually be MOST serious in the

   A. summer    B. fall    C. spring    D. winter

32. When sheeting for a trench is not to be removed before backfilling, the sheeting should be driven or cut off so that it

   A. is flush with the surface of the ground
   B. is at least 8 inches below the surface of the ground

C. will project at least two inches into the pavement base
D. is flush with the top surface of the pavement base

33. While excavating a trench in rock by blasting, a water main which crosses the line of the trench is uncovered. Of the following methods, the BEST one for continuing the rock excavation in the vicinity of the main is

    A. shut down the main
    B. place blasting mats to cover the main
    C. use lighter blasting charges
    D. relocate the main temporarily so that it is outside the danger area of the building

34. When the bottom of a trench for a water main is in rock, the pipe should be permanently supported on

    A. clean earth backfill which is tamped
    B. wooden blocking
    C. sand backfill which is flushed
    D. concreted cradles

35. On which one of the following days of the week should a planned shutdown normally be made?

    A. Sunday         B. Monday
    C. Tuesday        D. Wednesday

36. Permissible leakage during a field test is two (2) gallons per linear foot of pipe joint per 24 hours.
    For a 24-inch main, 1,000 feet long, with 16-foot laying lengths, the permissible leakage in 24 hours is, in gallons, MOST NEARLY

    A. 750    B. 770    C. 790    D. 810

37. Contract limitations on the maximum quantities of materials that may be delivered to the site, and on the time of such deliveries, are USUALLY made in order to

    A. insure the completion of the work on schedule
    B. prevent the contractor from asking for an extension of time because materials were not available
    C. reduce congestion at the site of the work
    D. protect the manufacturer supplying the material

38. Steel reinforcing bars for reinforced concrete should

    A. be painted with red lead
    B. be painted with asphalt paint
    C. be painted with oil paint
    D. not be painted

39. Steel water mains are lined with

    A. coal tar enamel only
    B. coal tar enamel or cement mortar
    C. cement mortar only
    D. nothing

40. The principal danger in NOT opening an air cock when draining a main is that the main might

    A. not empty
    B. only partly empty
    C. empty too fast
    D. collapse

---

# KEY (CORRECT ANSWERS)

| | | | | | | | |
|---|---|---|---|---|---|---|---|
| 1. | C | 11. | C | 21. | B | 31. | D |
| 2. | B | 12. | A | 22. | C | 32. | B |
| 3. | D | 13. | A | 23. | A | 33. | D |
| 4. | A | 14. | D | 24. | C | 34. | D |
| 5. | C | 15. | C | 25. | B | 35. | D |
| 6. | D | 16. | B | 26. | A | 36. | C |
| 7. | A | 17. | A | 27. | A | 37. | C |
| 8. | C | 18. | D | 28. | C | 38. | D |
| 9. | D | 19. | D | 29. | A | 39. | B |
| 10. | D | 20. | B | 30. | C | 40. | D |

---

# EXAMINATION SECTION
# TEST 1

DIRECTIONS: Each question or incomplete statement is followed by several suggested answers or completions. Select the one that BEST answers the question or completes the statement. *PRINT THE LETTER OF THE CORRECT ANSWER IN THE SPACE AT THE RIGHT.*

1. When filling an empty aqueduct, the valve should be opened

    A. slowly to prevent damage to the aqueduct
    B. rapidly to fill the line as soon as possible
    C. slowly to prevent rapid lowering of the reservoir level
    D. rapidly so that there are no air locks

2. The BEST way of detecting the location of a suspected chlorine leak is by placing a _____ near the suspected leak.

    A. rag, which has been dipped in a strong ammonia water,
    B. match
    C. piece of litmus paper
    D. flow meter

3. The term *run-off* refers to the

    A. amount a valve must be turned in order to open it fully
    B. length of time an electric motor continues to turn after the current is shut off
    C. amount of rainfall which flows from the ground surface into the streams and reservoirs
    D. distance the water falls from the intake gate to the turbine

4. Algae in reservoirs may be killed by using

    A. zeolite           B. copper sulphate
    C. sodium chloride   D. calcium chloride

5. The one of the following types of valves that USUALLY operates without manual control is a(n) _____ valve.

    A. check       B. globe       C. gate       D. angle

6. Rate of flow of water through a water treatment plant is USUALLY referred to in terms of

    A. c.f.s.      B. c.f.m.      C. r.p.m.     D. m.g.d.

7. In order to make it easier to operate a large valve or gate, pressures on both sides of the valve or gate are balanced by

    A. using weights on each side of the valve or gate
    B. opening a smaller by-pass valve
    C. partially shutting down the water in the upstream line
    D. opening the downstream valve very slowly

8. Leaves are removed from the water entering the treatment plant or aqueduct by

    A. skimming    B. coagulating    C. draining    D. screening

9. Odors, due to gases in the water, are removed by

   A. surging  B. sluicing  C. aerating  D. clarifying

10. Chlorine residual refers to the

    A. amount of chlorine that must be added to the water
    B. amount of chlorine that remains in the water after a given period
    C. method of adding the chlorine to the water
    D. method of protecting personnel using chlorine from the effects of the chlorine

11. One of the processes that takes place in an Imhoff tank is

    A. oxidation  B. flocculation  C. digestion  D. coagulation

12. As used in a sewage disposal plant, *effluent* refers to the

    A. basic treatment process of sewage
    B. time it takes for complete treatment of sewage
    C. type of control the plant uses for treatment
    D. final liquid coming out of the treatment process

13. A grit chamber operates on the basis that

    A. grit will settle out of slow-moving water
    B. grit will float and can be removed by skimming the surface
    C. increasing the rate of flow of water will leave the grit behind
    D. spraying water into the air will cause the heavier grit to separate from the water

14. The purpose of sedimentation in any sewage treatment process is to

    A. aerate the sewage
    B. increase the chlorine content of the sewage
    C. remove suspended matter from the sewage
    D. kill the bacteria in the sewage

15. The final treatment for sludge before it is disposed of is

    A. drying                B. adding chlorine
    C. mixing                D. washing

16. The amount of sewage applied to a filter bed is GENERALLY controlled by a

    A. sluice gate           B. flow meter
    C. dosing siphon         D. regulating valve

17. Methane gas which results from the sewage treatment process is MOST frequently

    A. vented to the outside air to prevent injury to plant personnel
    B. used as a fuel in the plant
    C. combined with other gases to render it harmless
    D. burned in the open air

18. The filtering material in a *filter bed* at a sewage treat- ment plant is USUALLY

    A. activated charcoal    B. sand
    C. alum                  D. ammonium chloride

19. Cleaning sewer lines is USUALLY done by the use of a

    A. catch basin          B. flushometer
    C. sewer rod            D. center line

20. One of the ways of locating a leak in a water line is by using a

    A. manometer           B. sounding rod
    C. poling board        D. diffusor

21. MOST sewer pipes are made of

    A. cast iron           B. agricultural tile
    C. brass               D. copper

22. One of the materials generally used in caulking joints in bell and spigot pipe is

    A. tar     B. litharge     C. red lead     D. oakum

23. Water pipe must be laid at least two feet below the ground surface MAINLY to

    A. prevent freezing
    B. discourage malicious tampering
    C. reduce the pressure required to make the water flow
    D. eliminate possibility of damage to roads in case of water main break

24. When soldering copper gutters, the flux that is GENERALLY used is

    A. sal ammoniac        B. resin
    C. killed muriatic acid D. calcium chloride

25. A good concrete mix for use in the foundations of a small building is

    A. 1:2:5     B. 5:2:1     C. 2:5:1     D. 1:5:2

26. When painting steel, red lead is used MAINLY as a

    A. primer coat so final coat will adhere better
    B. primer coat to protect the steel from rusting
    C. finish coat to protect the steel from the action of the sun and water
    D. second coat to bind the primer and finish coats

27. Studs in frame buildings are USUALLY

    A. 1" x 4"    B. 1" x 6"    C. 2" x 4"    D. 2" x 6"

28. A cement mortar used in brickwork is USUALLY made more workable by adding

    A. phosphate    B. lime    C. calcium    D. grout

Questions 29-32.

DIRECTIONS: The following four questions numbered 29 to 32, inclusive, are to be answered in accordance with the rules of the department of water supply, gas and electricity.

29. The term *water course* refers to

   A. aqueducts only
   B. pipe lines only
   C. natural or artificial streams only
   D. all of the above

30. Where a swimming pool discharges upon or into the ground and the water is not treated, the minimum distance between such discharge and a stream MUST be at least _____ feet.

   A. 50   B. 100   C. 250   D. 450

31. According to the above rules, clothes may

   A. be washed in a spring, if the spring does not feed directly into a reservoir
   B. be washed in a spring if the place where this is being done is at least one mile from a reservoir
   C. be washed in a spring provided a chlorinated soap is used
   D. not be washed in a spring

32. Industrial wastes may

   A. be discharged into a stream provided the stream does not feed directly into a reservoir
   B. be discharged into a stream, provided the point of discharge is at least one mile from a reservoir
   C. be discharged into a stream if the wastes are purified in an approved manner
   D. not be discharged into a stream

33. One method of determining the height of the water in a stream feeding into a reservoir is by means of a

   A. venturi meter        B. flow meter
   C. hook gage            D. strain gage

34. When digging a deep trench, the sides are USUALLY prevented from caving in by using

   A. shoulders   B. blocking   C. pins   D. sheathing

35. The FIRST precaution a worker should take before entering a sewer manhole is to

   A. put on hard-toed shoes
   B. put on safety goggles
   C. check that the next manhole upstream is not obstructed
   D. test the air in the manhole

36. Assume that a fuse blows upon connecting a light load to the circuit. You replace it with the same size fuse, and again the fuse blows.
    The BEST thing to do in this case is to

   A. connect a wire across the fuse so it cannot blow under such a light load
   B. replace the fuse with one having a higher rating
   C. check the wiring of the circuit
   D. place two fuses in series to prevent blowing

37. Of the following material, the one that is BEST for fill as a subgrade for a road is            37.____

    A. sand
    B. silt
    C. clay
    D. a mixture of sand, silt, and clay

38. When dealing with leaking chlorine, it is IMPORTANT to remember that chlorine is           38.____

    A. highly flammable
    B. made safe by spraying water on it
    C. not corrosive
    D. heavier than air

39. Cast iron pipe is MOST frequently cut with a(n)           39.____

    A. hack saw                 B. diamond point chisel
    C. burning torch            D. abrasive wheel

40. Water hammer in a pipe line is BEST reduced by installing           40.____

    A. a pressure regulator
    B. an air chamber
    C. smaller pipes and valves
    D. larger pipes and valves

---

## KEY (CORRECT ANSWERS)

| | | | | | | | |
|---|---|---|---|---|---|---|---|
| 1. | A | 11. | C | 21. | A | 31. | D |
| 2. | A | 12. | D | 22. | D | 32. | D |
| 3. | C | 13. | A | 23. | A | 33. | C |
| 4. | B | 14. | C | 24. | C | 34. | D |
| 5. | A | 15. | A | 25. | A | 35. | D |
| 6. | D | 16. | C | 26. | B | 36. | C |
| 7. | B | 17. | B | 27. | C | 37. | D |
| 8. | D | 18. | B | 28. | B | 38. | D |
| 9. | C | 19. | C | 29. | D | 39. | B |
| 10. | B | 20. | B | 30. | B | 40. | B |

# TEST 2

DIRECTIONS: Each question or incomplete statement is followed by several suggested answers or completions. Select the one that BEST answers the question or completes the statement. *PRINT THE LETTER OF THE CORRECT ANSWER IN SPACE AT THE RIGHT.*

1. When used in conjunction with a centrifugal pump, a foot valve                1.____

   A. equalizes the pressure on both sides of the pump
   B. regulates the amount of water flowing through the pump
   C. prevents water in the pump from flowing back down the suction line
   D. adjusts the speed of the pump to the amount of water to be pumped

2. Grounding an electric motor is                2.____

   A. *good* practice because the motor will operate better
   B. *poor* practice because the motor will not operate as well
   C. *good* practice because it protects against shock hazards
   D. *poor* practice because it increases shock hazards

3. The one of the following wrenches that should NOT be used to turn a nut is a ____ wrench.                3.____

   A. monkey        B. box        C. stillson        D. socket

4. A drill is GENERALLY removed from the chuck of a portable electric drill by using a                4.____

   A. drift pin            B. wedge
   C. centerpunch          D. key

5. The finished surface of a dirt road is MOST frequently maintained with a                5.____

   A. blade grader         B. bulldozer
   C. dragline             D. carryall

6. Frequent stalling of a truck engine is MOST probably due to a                6.____

   A. weak battery         B. low battery water level
   C. leaking oil filter   D. dirty carburetor

7. If the reading of the oil pressure gage on a gasoline motor should suddenly drop to zero, the FIRST thing the operator should do is to                7.____

   A. check the filter
   B. inspect the oil lines
   C. tighten the oil pan bolts
   D. stop the motor

8. A tractor is to be stored for two months. In order to keep it in BEST condition, it should be                8.____

   A. drained of all fuel and oil
   B. lubricated every week
   C. started up periodically and run until warm
   D. steam cleaned and all water drained from the radiator

9. Trees suffering from transplanting shock are quickly helped by                9.____

A. deep watering  B. foliage feeding
C. root feeding   D. vitamin treatments

10. For MOST rapid healing, trees should be pruned during

    A. November, December, and January
    B. February, March, and April
    C. May, June, and July
    D. August, September, and October

11. The blades of a lawn mower should be set so that the blades

    A. firmly touch the bed knife
    B. barely touch the bed knife
    C. clear the bed knife by 1/16 inch
    D. clear the bed knife by 1/8 inch

12. The MAIN reason for mulching is to

    A. fertilize the soil
    B. prevent erosion
    C. protect plants from the cold
    D. kill insects

13. A compost heap would MOST likely include

    A. lawn clippings     B. sand
    C. stumps of trees    D. gravel

14. Of the following statements with regard to *seeding,* the one that is CORRECT is:

    A. Seeds should be sown on a windy day
    B. The ground should be watered heavily after seeding
    C. Seeding should be done primarily on a bright and sunny day
    D. It is not necessary to carefully apportion the amount of seeds sown

15. Organic matter is often added to soil to better condition it for growing plants. Of the following, the item that is NOT organic matter is

    A. lime    B. peat    C. manure    D. leaf mold

16. Of the following, the BEST way to store coniferous seedlings which cannot be planted for a few days is to

    A. unwrap them and put them in a dark, dry location
    B. place them flat on the ground in a sunny location so they can get plenty of light and air
    C. place them in a trench dug in the earth and cover the root ends with soil
    D. make sure the ball is not loosened and keep in a hothouse

17. Transplanting of seedlings is BEST done in early

    A. spring    B. summer    C. autumn    D. winter

18. After planting privet hedges, they are frequently cut back to within a few inches of the ground.
This is USUALLY done to

    A. remove dead parts of the hedge
    B. insure dense growth from the ground up
    C. speed up root development
    D. reduce the possibility of insect damage while the hedge is taking root

19. *Heaving* of pavements in wintertime is USUALLY caused by the

    A. difference of expansion of pavement and subgrade
    B. freezing of water in subgrade
    C. loss of bond between pavement and subgrade
    D. brittleness of pavement

20. Erosion of side slopes caused by the action of water is GREATEST when the soil is

    A. silt    B. clay    C. hardpan    D. silty-clay

21. The MAIN reason for making a crown in a road pavement is to

    A. reduce the amount of paving material necessary
    B. make it easier for cars to go around a curve
    C. drain surface water
    D. increase the strength of the pavement where it is most needed

22. The MAIN reason for paving ditches at the side of a road is to

    A. prevent damage from cars
    B. permit the ditch to carry more water
    C. prevent erosion of the soil in the ditch
    D. block water from getting under the pavement

23. Assume that vitrified clay tile pipe, with open joints, is being used as the underdrain for a roadway.
This pipe should be laid

    A. directly on the bottom of the trench
    B. on a bed of clay
    C. on a bed of peat
    D. on a bed of gravel

24. A macadam road is one in which the base is GENERALLY made of

    A. asphalt           B. broken stone
    C. concrete          D. stabilized soil

25. To loosen compacted rocky earth road surfaces, the BEST piece of equipment to use is a

    A. disc harrow    B. drag line    C. bulldozer    D. scarifier

26. Oiling of an earth road is BEST done

    A. in the winter before the snow falls
    B. when you expect much rain

C. in the spring during dry weather
D. immediately after snow is cleared from the road

27. Cracks in concrete roads are BEST repaired by filling them with 27.____

    A. tar          B. grout
    C. mineral filler   D. sand

28. When repairing patches in old asphalt pavements, the edges of the patch should FIRST be painted with 28.____

    A. the same material used for the patch
    B. kerosene
    C. asphalt cement
    D. asphalt binder

29. The sum of 3 1/4, 5 1/8, 2 1/2, and 3 3/8 is 29.____

    A. 14      B. 14 1/8     C. 14 1/4     D. 14 3/8

30. Assume that it takes 6 men 8 days to do a particular job. 30.____
    If you have only 4 men available to do this job and they all work at the same speed, then the number of days it would take to complete the job would be

    A. 11      B. 12      C. 13      D. 14

31. The city aims to supply *potable* water. As used in this sentence, the word *potable* means MOST NEARLY 31.____

    A. clear   B. drinkable   C. fresh   D. adequate

32. Water, after being purified, should not be turbid. As used in this sentence, the word turbid means MOST NEARLY 32.____

    A. cloudy   B. warm   C. infected   D. hard

33. The flow of water is *impeded* by the silt in the bottom of the stream. 33.____
    As used in this sentence, the word *impeded* means MOST NEARLY

    A. dammed   B. hindered   C. helped   D. dirtied

Questions 34-35.

DIRECTIONS: Questions 34 and 35 are based on the following paragraph.

*Repeated burning of the same area should be avoided. Burning should not be done on impervious, shallow, unstable, or highly erodible soils, or on steep slopes - especially in areas subject to heavy rains or rapid snowmelt. When existing vegetation is likely to be killed or seriously weakened by the fire, measures should be taken to assure prompt revegetation of the burned area. Burns should be limited to relatively small proportions of a watershed unit so that the stream channels will be able to carry any increased flows with a minimum of damage.*

34. According to the above paragraph, planned burning should be limited to small areas of the watershed because

   A. the fire can be better controlled
   B. existing vegetation will be less likely to be killed
   C. plants will grow quicker in small areas
   D. there will be less likelihood of damaging floods

35. According to the above paragraph, burning usually should be done on soils that

   A. readily absorb moisture
   B. have been burnt before
   C. exist as a thin layer over rock
   D. can be flooded by nearby streams

36. If a foreman does not understand the instructions that are given to him by the district engineer, the BEST thing to do is to

   A. work out the solution to the problem himself
   B. do the job in the way he thinks is best
   C. get one of the other foremen to do the job
   D. ask that the instructions be repeated and clarified

37. The BEST foreman is the one who

   A. can work as fast as the fastest man in the crew
   B. is the most skilled mechanic
   C. can get the most work out of the men
   D. is the strongest man

38. Complimenting a man for good work is

   A. *good* practice since it will give the man an incentive to continue working well
   B. *poor* practice because the other men will become jealous
   C. *good* practice because in the future the foreman will not have to supervise this man
   D. *poor* practice since the man should work well without needing compliments

39. In dealing with his men, it is MOST important that a foreman be

   A. a disciplinarian        B. stern
   C. fair                    D. chummy with his men

40. When issuing a violation to a member of the public, it is MOST important that a foreman be

   A. aloof and refuse to discuss the violation
   B. stern, and warn the person to correct the violation immediately
   C. courteous and explain what must be done to correct the violation
   D. friendly and volunteer assistance to correct the violation

## KEY (CORRECT ANSWERS)

| | | | |
|---|---|---|---|
| 1. C | 11. B | 21. C | 31. B |
| 2. C | 12. C | 22. C | 32. A |
| 3. C | 13. A | 23. D | 33. B |
| 4. D | 14. B | 24. B | 34. D |
| 5. A | 15. A | 25. D | 35. A |
| 6. D | 16. C | 26. C | 36. D |
| 7. D | 17. A | 27. A | 37. C |
| 8. C | 18. B | 28. C | 38. A |
| 9. B | 19. B | 29. C | 39. C |
| 10. B | 20. A | 30. B | 40. C |

# EXAMINATION SECTION
## TEST 1

DIRECTIONS: Each question or incomplete statement is followed by several suggested answers or completions. Select the one that *BEST* answers the question or completes the statement. *PRINT THE LETTER OF THE CORRECT ANSWER IN THE SPACE AT THE RIGHT.*

1. Cold waterpipes in buildings are insulated *MAINLY* in order to

    A. prevent the accumulation of static electricity in the pipes
    B. prevent condensation of water from the air on the pipes
    C. reduce expansion of the pipes
    D. reduce water hammer

2. A valve that *automatically* closes to prevent the flow of water in the opposite direction is a

    A. check valve           B. globe valve
    C. gate valve            D. corporation cock

3. A connection between two pipes in the same water-supply system or between two water-supply systems containing potable water is called a

    A. spillway              B. cross connection
    C. crossover             D. interconnection

4. Asbestos cement water pipes are *usually* connected by

    A. victaulic couplings
    B. sweated couplings
    C. dresser couplings
    D. two rubber rings and a sleeve

5. Of the following types of pipes, the *one* that should *NOT* be used on hot water lines is

    A. brass                 B. copper
    C. galvanized iron       D. lead

6. Potable water begins to freeze when the temperature falls to

    A. 4° F      B. 20° F      C. 32° F      D. 48° F

7. The travel of mice through pipe openings in walls and floors is *usually* prevented by the use of a(n)

    A. plug      B. escutcheon      C. bonnet      D. blind flange

8. A water closet *usually* contains a

    A. corporation cock      B. pet cock
    C. ball cock             D. air cock

9. Before a worker pours lead in a bell-and-spigot joint, he should *FIRST* check to see that the joint is clean and

    A. lubricated      B. rough      C. hot      D. dry

10. Sweated joints are *most often* used in water systems on

   A. aluminum tubing  B. steel tubing
   C. malleable iron tubing  D. copper tubing

11. The type of paint which should *NOT* be used on surfaces in contact with potable water is

   A. zinc   B. enamel   C. asphaltum   D. silicate

12. Grade AA water service pipe is made of

   A. copper   B. lead   C. wrought iron   D. aluminum

13. When a new water meter is put into service care should be taken to displace the air in the meter *slowly* with water because

   A. rapid entry of water could damage the meter by water hammer
   B. air in the meter will cause it to under-register the amount of water actually flowing
   C. the air may cause self-siphonabe in the meter
   D. the rapid change in temperature caused by the surge of water will warp the disc

14. The pipe cross shown above is *propevly* specified as a

   A. 3x4x2x3 cross   B. 2x3x3x4 cross
   C. 4x3x3x2 cross   D. 5x2x3x4 cross

15. In some plumbing lines when a faucet is closed suddenly, a noise is heard in the pipeline. This noise is known as water

   A. ram   B. hammer   C. knock   D. slug

16. A tailpiece is *most often* used in connection with piping for a

   A. sink drain   B. water closet flush tank
   C. water meter by pass   D. hose bibb

17. A plain round steel plate bolted at the end of a flanged steel pipe is known as a(n)

   A. companion flange   B. blind flange
   C. adapter flange   D. plug flange

18. A fitting that uses a water seal to prevent air and gas from passing through a drain line is called a

   A. vent   B. vacuum breaker
   C. tapped tee   D. trap

19. According to the building code, a steel gravity water storage tank placed outside a building

   A. may be painted on the outside only
   B. must be painted on the inside only
   C. should not be painted at all
   D. must be painted on both inside and outside

20. A hydropneumatic water system *usually* has a

   A. vacuum pump
   B. compressor
   C. steam engine
   D. hydraulic ram

21. A coating of rust on a steel pipe will

   A. accelerate further corrosion of the pipe
   B. check further corrosion of the pipe caused by rusting
   C. have no effect on the rate of corrosion of the pipe
   D. cause the pipe to deteriorate rapidly from direct oxidation

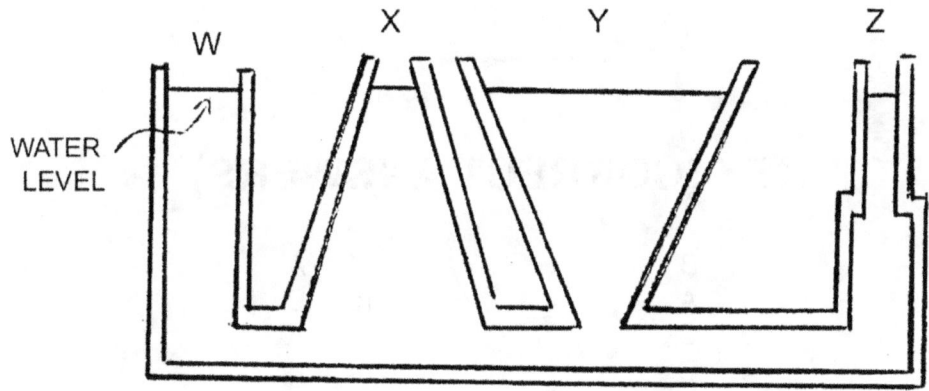

22. With reference to the tank shown in the above diagram, the statement that is *true* is that

   A. Section Z will have the highest water level
   B. the water pressure at the bottom of Section Y will be greater than the water pressure at the bottom of Section X
   C. Section Z will have the lowest water level
   D. the water pressure at the bottom of Section Y is equal to the water pressure at the bottom of Section X

23. The condition of water seeping from a water main through poorly constructed joints is called

   A. infiltration
   B. leakage
   C. cavitation
   D. percolation

24. A 1/8 bend cast-iron fitting will alter the direction of flow in a water main

   A. 22 1/2°　　B. 45°　　C. 90°　　D. 135°

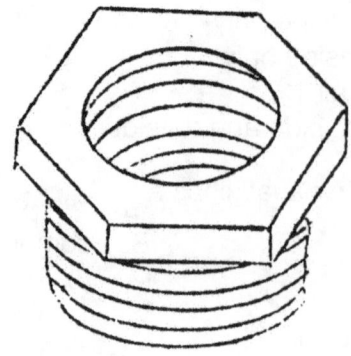

25. The fitting represented in the above drawing is known as a
   A. nipple
   B. hexagonal insert
   C. bushing
   D. reducer

25.____

---

## KEY (CORRECT ANSWERS)

| | | | |
|---|---|---|---|
| 1. | B | 11. | A |
| 2. | A | 12. | B |
| 3. | C | 13. | A |
| 4. | D | 14. | C |
| 5. | D | 15. | B |
| 6. | C | 16. | A |
| 7. | B | 17. | B |
| 8. | C | 18. | D |
| 9. | D | 19. | D |
| 10. | D | 20. | B |

21. B
22. D
23. B
24. B
25. C

---

# TEST 2

DIRECTIONS: Each question or incomplete statement is followed by several suggested answers or completions. Select the one that BEST answers the question or completes the Statement. *PRINT THE LETTER OF THE CORRECT ANSWER IN THE SPACE AT THE EIGHT.*

1. Solder for wiping joints is an alloy MAINLY made up of

    A. copper and lead
    B. lead and tin
    C. lead and zinc
    D. copper and zinc

2. A short piece of pipe, threaded on the outside only, used for connecting pipes or fittings in threaded joints, is known as a

    A. ferrule   B. bushing   C. coupling   D. nipple

3. Burrs inside of a steel pipe are BEST removed with a

    A. gouge   B. rasp   C. blivet   D. reamer

4. The symbol ⟶✗⟶ on a plumbing diagram represents a

    A. flanged joint
    B. screwed joint
    C. bell-and-spigot joint
    D. welded joint

5. The symbol ⟶⋈⟶ on a plumbing diagram represents a

    A. gate valve
    B. angle valve
    C. swing valve
    D. globe valve

6. The PROPER wrench to use to tighten a pipe that has a finished outside surface, so that the surface is not scratched, is a

    A. Stillson wrench
    B. strap wrench
    C. chain wrench
    D. monkey wrench

7. Brass is an alloy made up MAINLY of copper and

    A. zinc   B. steel   C. lead   D. aluminum

8. Of the following, the BEST reason for specifying that water service pipe be buried at least 4 feet below surface of the ground is that

    A. water service pipe is very strong
    B. the amount of excavation will be reduced
    C. water will be prevented from freezing in the pipe
    D. it is easier to install that way

9. Of the following joints, the *one* which should NOT be used on the outlet side of a trap is a

    A. flanged joint
    B. slip joint
    C. screwed joint
    D. welded joint

10. When thawing a frozen water supply pipe, it is BEST to start

   A. in the middle, with the faucet closed, and work outwards in both directions so that the thawing is as uniform as possible
   B. on the supply side first, with the faucet closed, to maintain pressure to melt the ice
   C. on the supply side first, with the faucet open, to permit steam to escape
   D. on the outlet side first with the faucet open

11. In plumbing word, a "sizing tool" is used MAINLY to

   A. flare the end of copper tubing for a compression type copper fitting
   B. cut copper tubing to size
   C. prevent kinks when bending copper tubing
   D. remove burrs from copper tubing

12. According to the current building code, caulking ferrules should be made of brass or

   A. copper              B. aluminum
   C. bronze              D. malleable iron

13. According to the current building code, horizontal copper tubing (1 1/4" or less) should be supported at intervals of *not greater than*

   A. 5 ft.      B. 3. 6 ft.      C. 7 ft.      D. 8 ft.

14. According to the current building code, the minimum flow rate for a 1/2" sink faucet should be *not less than*

   A. 2.5 gpm    B. 3.5 gpm    C. 4.5 gpm    D. 5.5 gpm

15. According to the current building code, when color-marking is used, non-potable water lines should be painted

   A. orange     B. yellow     C. red        D. green

16. A specification states that water for concrete shall be clean and free from INJURIOUS amounts of oil, alkali, organic or other foreign substances.
    In the above statement the word INJURIOUS means

   A. harmful    B. tonic      C. good       D. sanitary

17. A specification states that hose lines shall be made up of 25-foot lengths or 50-foot lengths, only one of which may be a 25-foot length, except that when more than 25 feet and less than 50 feet is required, the hose shall be in one section of the required length. No length may be less than 25 feet long.
    According to the above passage, the number of lengths of hose that can be used to make up a hose 265 feet long is

   A. 4          B. 5          C. 6          D. 7

18. A specification states that control valves 2" and smaller shall be OS & I bronze gate valves.
    In the above statement, the abbreviation OS & Y means

A. Outside Screw and Yardarm
B. Outside Screw and Yoke
C. Outside Seal and Yarn
D. Outside Spring and Y-handle

19. A specification states that contact type energy cut-off devices shall be *RIGIDLY* mounted in contact with the shell of the water heater.
As used in the above statement, the word *RIGIDLY* means

A. firmly   B. flexibly   C. limberly   D. loosely

19._____

Question 20.

DIRECTIONS: Answer Question 20 on the basis of the paragraph below.

Experience has shown that, in general, a result of the installation of meters on services not previously metered is to reduce the amount of water consumed, but is not necessarily to reduce the peak load on plumbing systems. The permissible head loss through meters at their rated maximum flow is 20 psi. The installation of a meter may therefore appreciably lower the pressures available in fixtures on a plumbing system.

20. According to the above paragraph, a water meter may

A. limit the flow in the plumbing system of 20 psi
B. reduce the peak load on the plumbing system
C. increase the overall amount of water consumed
D. reduce the pressure in the plumbing system

20._____

21. The toilet has a flushing mechanism made entirely of non-corrosive COMPONENTS.
In the above statement, the word COMPONENTS means

A. aggregates   B. parts   C. totals   D. masses

21._____

Questions 22 - 24.

DIRECTIONS: Answer Questions 22 to 24 on the basis of the passage below.

Gas heaters include manually operated, automatic, and instantaneous heaters. Some heaters are equipped with a thermostat which controls the fuel supply so that when the *water* falls below a predetermined temperature, the fuel is automatically turned on. In some types the hot-water storage tank is well-insulated to economize the use of fuel. Instantaneous heaters are arranged so that the opening of a faucet on the hot-water pipe will increase the flow of fuel, which is ignited by a continuously burning pilot light to heat the water to from 120 to 130ºF. The possibility that the pilot light will die out offers a source of danger in the use of automatic appliances which depend on a pilot light. Gas and oil heaters are dangerous, and they should be designed to prevent the accumulation, in a confined space within the heater, of a large volume of an explosive mixture.

22. According to the above passage, the opening of a hot-water faucet on a hot-water pipe connected to an instantaneous hot-water heater will

    A. *increase* the temperature of the pilot light
    B. *increase* the flow of fuel to the pilot light
    C. *decrease* the flow of fuel to the pilot light
    D. *have a marked effect* on the pilot light

23. According to the above passage, the fuel is automatically turned on in a heater equipped with a thermostat whenever

    A. the water temperature drops below 120° F
    B. the pilot light is lit
    C. the water temperature drops below some predetermined temperature
    D. a hot water supply is opened

24. According to the above passage, some hot-water storage tanks are well-insulated to

    A. accelerate the burning of the fuel
    B. maintain the water temperature between 120° and 130°F
    C. prevent the pilot light from being extinguished
    D. minimize the expenditure of fuel

Question 25.

DIRECTIONS: Answer Question 25 on the basis of the passage below.

Breakage of the piston under high-speed operation has been the commonest fault of disc piston meters. Various techniques are adopted to prevent this, such as *THROTTLING* the meter, cutting away the edge of the piston, or reinforcing it but these are simply makeshifts.

25. As used in the above passage, the word *THROTTLING* means most nearly

    A. enlarging         B. choking
    C. harnessing        D. dismantling

## KEY (CORRECT ANSWERS)

1. B
2. D
3. D
4. D
5. A

6. B
7. A
8. C
9. B
10. D

11. A
12. A
13. B
14. C
15. B

16. A
17. C
18. B
19. A
20. D

21. B
22. B
23. C
24. D
25. B

# EXAMINATION SECTION
# TEST 1

DIRECTIONS: Each question or incomplete statement is followed by several suggested answers or completions. Select the one that BEST answers the question or completes the statement. *PRINT THE LETTER OF THE CORRECT ANSWER IN THE SPACE AT THE RIGHT.*

Questions 1-2.

DIRECTIONS: Questions 1 and 2 are to be answered on the basis of the passage below.

When summers are hot and dry, much water will be used for watering lawns. Domestic use will be further increased by more bathing, while public use will be affected by much street sprinkling and use in parks and recreation fields for watering grass and for ornamental fountains. Variations in the weather may cause variations in water consumption. A succession of showers in the summer could significantly reduce water consumption. High temperatures may also lead to high water use for air-conditioning purposes. On the other hand, in cold weather, water may be wasted at the faucets to prevent freezing of pipes, thereby greatly increasing consumption.

1. According to the above passage, water consumption

    A. will not be affected by the weather to any appreciable extent
    B. will always increase in the warm weather and decrease in cold weather
    C. will increase in cold weather and decrease in warm weather
    D. may increase because of high or low temperatures

1.____

2. The MAIN subject of the above passage is:

    A. Climatic conditions affecting water consumption
    B. Water consumption in arid regions
    C. Conservation of water
    D. Weather variations

2.____

Questions 3-4.

DIRECTIONS: Questions 3 and 4 are to be answered on the basis of the passage below.

The efficiency of the water works management will affect consumption by decreasing loss and waste. Leaks in the water mains and services and unauthorized use of water can be kept to a minimum by surveys. A water supply that is both safe and attractive in quality will be used to a greater extent than one of poor quality. In this connection, it should be recognized that improvement of the quality of water supply will probably be followed by an increase in consumption. Increasing the pressure will have a similar effect. Changing the rates charged for water will also affect consumption. A study found that consumption decreases about five percent for each ten percent increase in water rates. Similarly, water consumption increases when the water rates are decreasing.

3. According to the above passage, an increase in the quality of water would MOST likely

   A. cause an increase in water consumption
   B. decrease water consumption by about 10%
   C. cause a decrease in water consumption
   D. have no effect on water consumption

4. According to the above passage, a ten percent decrease in water rates would MOST likely result in a _____ percent _____ in the water consumption.

   A. five; decrease
   B. five; increase
   C. ten; decrease
   D. ten; increase

Questions 5-6.

DIRECTIONS: Questions 5 and 6 are to be answered on the basis of the passage below.

While the average domestic use of water may be expected to be about 35 gallons per person daily, wide variations are found. These are largely dependent upon the economic status of the consumers and will differ greatly in various sections of the city. In the high value residential districts of a city or in a suburban community of similar type population, the water consumption per person will be high. In apartment houses, which may be considered as representing the maximum domestic demand to be expected, the average consumption should be about 60 gallons per person. In an area of high value single residences, even higher consumption may be expected, since to the ordinary domestic demand there will be added amount for watering lawns. The slum districts of large cities will show a consumption per person of about 20 gallons daily. The lowest figures of all will be found in low value districts, where sewerage is not available and where perhaps a single faucet serves one or several households.

5. According to the above passage, domestic water consumption per person

   A. would probably be lowest for persons in an area of high value single residences
   B. would probably be lowest for persons in an apartment house
   C. would probably be lowest for persons in a slum area
   D. does not depend at all upon area or income

6. According to the above passage, the water consumption in apartment houses as compared to slum houses is about _____ times as much.

   A. 1 1/2    B. 2    C. 2 1/2    D. 3

Questions 7-8.

DIRECTIONS: Questions 7 and 8 are to be answered on the basis of the passage below.

One of the greatest hazards to an industrial plant is fire. Consequently, a rigid system should be set up for periodic inspection of all types of fire protective equipment. Such inspections should include water tanks, sprinkler systems, standpipes, hose, fire plugs, extinguishers, and all other equipment used for fire protection. The schedule of inspections should be closely followed and an ACCURATE record kept of each piece of equipment inspected and tested.

Along with this scheduled inspection, a careful survey should be made of new equipment needed. Recommendations should be made for replacement of defective and obsolete equipment, as well as the purchase of any additional equipment. As new processes and products are added to the manufacturing system, new fire hazards may be introduced that require individual treatment and possible special extinguishing devices. Plant inspection personnel should be sure to follow through.

Surveys should also include all means of egress from the building. Exits, stairs, fire towers, fire escapes, halls, fire alarm systems, emergency lighting systems, and places seldom used should be thoroughly inspected to determine their adequacy and readiness for emergency use.

7. Of the following titles, the one that BEST fits the above passage is:

   A. NEW, USED, AND OLD FIRE PROTECTION EQUIPMENT
   B. MAINTENANCE OF FIRE PROTECTION EQUIPMENT
   C. INSPECTION OF FIRE PROTECTION EQUIPMENT
   D. OVERHAUL OF WORN OUT FIRE FIGHTING EQUIPMENT

8. As used in the above passage, the word ACCURATE means

   A. exact
   B. approximate
   C. close
   D. vague

9. In talking with a homeowner, an inspector should always be *polite*.
   As used in the above statement, the word *polite* means

   A. cold    B. courteous    C. aggressive    D. modest

10. In talking with a homeowner, an inspector should not discuss *trivial* matters.
    As used in the above statement, the word *trivial* means

    A. related
    B. essential
    C. significant
    D. unimportant

11. The one of the following words that is SIMILAR in meaning to *revise* is

    A. edit
    B. confuse
    C. complicate
    D. dismiss

12. The one of the following words that is SIMILAR in meaning to *abandon* is

    A. quit    B. use    C. remain    D. discourage

13. The one of the following words that is SIMILAR in meaning to *adjacent* is

    A. far    B. detached    C. bordering    D. distant

14. The one of the following words that is SIMILAR in meaning to *coarse* is

    A. fine    B. smooth    C. rough    D. slick

15. The one of the following words that is SIMILAR in meaning to *orifice* is

    A. chamber    B. enclosure    C. opening    D. device

16. The one of the following words that has the OPPOSITE meaning of *partition* is   16.___

    A. division  B. connection
    C. barrier   D. compartment

17. The one of the following words that has the OPPOSITE meaning of *obvious* is   17.___

    A. concealed  B. known  C. clear  D. apparent

18. The one of the following words that has the OPPOSITE meaning of *assist* is   18.___

    A. hinder  B. offer  C. demand  D. aid

19. The one of the following words that has the OPPOSITE meaning of *obsolete* is   19.___

    A. neglected  B. traditional
    C. rare       D. new

20. The one of the following words that has the OPPOSITE meaning of *stagnant* is   20.___

    A. murky  B. active  C. calm  D. dirty

21. The number of gallons of water contained in a cylindrical swimming pool 8 feet in diameter and filled to a depth of 3 feet 6 inches is MOST NEARLY (assume 7.5 gallons = 1 cubic foot)   21.___

    A. 30  B. 225  C. 1695  D. 3000

22. An inspector observes a meter reading of 02321 cu.ft. on a straight reading type of register. The previous reading on that meter for that location was 99332. The amount of water used between readings, assuming no backflow through the meter, was MOST NEARLY _____ cu.ft.   22.___

    A. -97511  B. 2489  C. 12489  D. 97511

Questions 23-24.

DIRECTIONS: Questions 23 and 24 are to be answered on the basis of the diagram of the dials of water meter shown below.

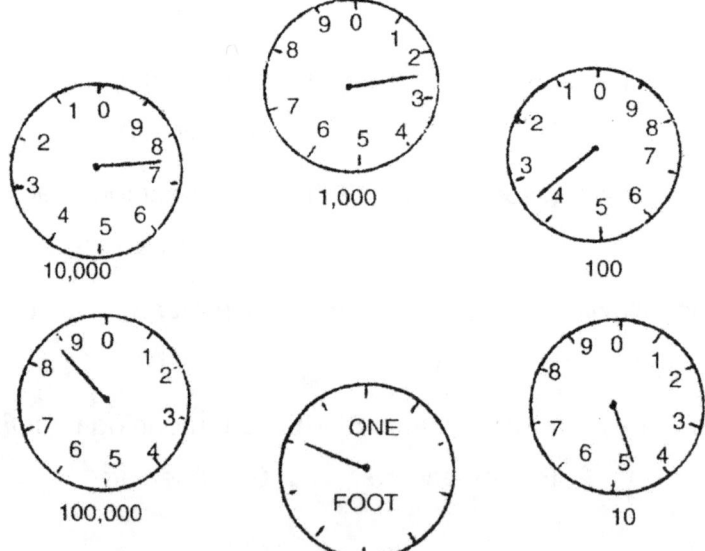

23. The CORRECT water meter reading, in cubic feet, is  23._____

   A. 43278   B. 54389   C. 87234   D. 98345

24. For each half revolution of the hand on the 10,000 dial, the hand on the indicator marked 10 will revolve _____ revolutions.  24._____

   A. 50   B. 500   C. 5,000   D. 50,000

25. If a 100-foot steel pipe expands 5/8 inch when the temperature rises 20° F, then the expansion of a steel pipe 40 feet long when the temperature rises 60° F is MOST NEARLY  25._____

   A. 1/2"   B. 5/8"   C. 3/4"   D. 7/8"

# KEY (CORRECT ANSWERS)

1. D   11. A
2. A   12. A
3. A   13. C
4. B   14. C
5. C   15. C

6. D   16. B
7. C   17. A
8. A   18. A
9. B   19. D
10. D  20. B

21. C
22. B
23. C
24. B
25. C

# TEST 2

DIRECTIONS: Each question or incomplete statement is followed by several suggested answers or completions. Select the one that BEST answers the question or completes the statement. *PRINT THE LETTER OF THE CORRECT ANSWER IN THE SPACE AT THE RIGHT.*

1.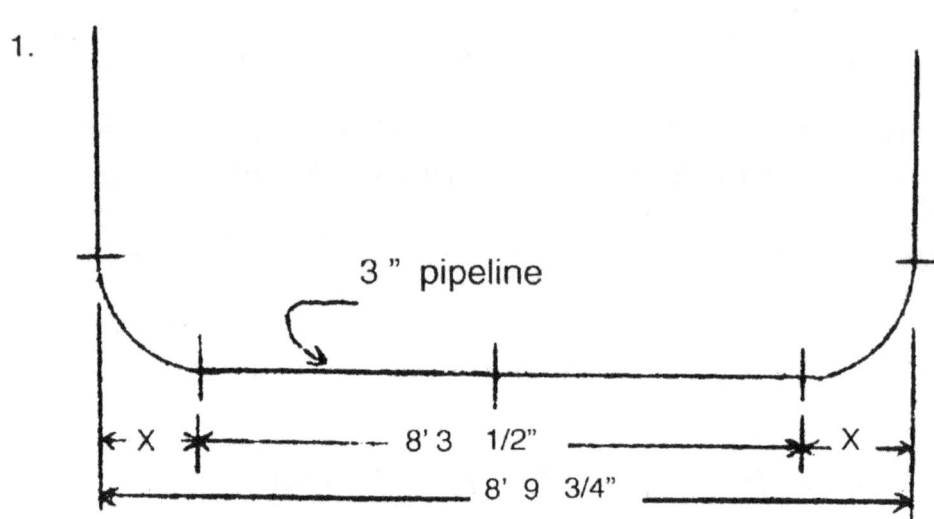

   In the above sketch of a 3" pipeline, the distance X is MOST NEARLY _____ inches.

   A.  3 1/8   B.  3 1/4   C.  3 1/2   D.  3 5/8

2. The fraction 9/64 is MOST NEARLY equal to

   A.  .1375   B.  .1406   C.  .1462   D.  .1489

3. The sum of the following dimensions is 1'2 3/6", 1'5 1/2", and 1'4 5/8" is

   A.  3'11 15/16"   B.  4'5/16"
   C.  4'11/16"      D.  4'1 5/8"

4. The scale on a plumbing drawing is 1/8" = 1 foot. A horizontal line measuring 3 5/16" on the drawing would represent a length of _____ feet.

   A.  24.9   B.  26.5   C.  28.3   D.  30.2

5. Assume that a water meter reads 50,631 cubic feet and the previous reading was 39,842 cubic feet.
   If the charge for water is 230 per 100 cubic feet or any fraction thereof, the bill for the amount of water used since the previous meter reading will be MOST NEARLY

   A.  $24.22   B.  $24.38   C.  $24.84   D.  $24.95

6. At a certain premises, the water consumption was 4 percent higher in 2005 than it was in 2004.
   If the water consumption for 2005 was 9740 cubic feet, then the water consumption for 2004 was MOST NEARLY _____ cubic feet.

   A.  9320   B.  9350   C.  9365   D.  9390

7. A pump delivers water at a constant rate of 40 gallons per minute. If there are 7.5 gallons to a cubic foot of water, the time it will take to fill a tank 6 ft. x 5 ft. x 4 ft. is MOST NEARLY _____ minutes.

   A. 15   B. 22.5   C. 28.5   D. 30

8. The total weight, in pounds, of three lengths of 3" cast iron pipe 7'6" long, weighing 14.5 pounds per foot, and four lengths of 4" cast iron pipe each 5'0" long, weighing 13.0 pounds per foot, is MOST NEARLY

   A. 540   B. 585   C. 600   D. 665

9. The water pressure at the bottom of a column of water 34 feet high is 14.7 lbs./sq.in. The water pressure, in lbs./sq.in., at the bottom of a column of water 12 feet high is MOST NEARLY

   A. 3   B. 5   C. 7   D. 9

10. The number of cubic yards of earth that would be removed when digging a trench 8 ft. wide x 9 ft. deep x 63 ft. long is

    A. 56   B. 168   C. 314   D. 504

11. If a newspaper man asks an inspector for facts about his job activities, the BEST of the following courses of action for the inspector to take is to

    A. be as evasive as possible
    B. refer him to the main office of the responsible department
    C. tell him everything off the record
    D. ignore the reporter altogether

12. Before entering a tightly covered water meter pit, it is MOST advisable for an inspector to FIRST

    A. remove pit cover and test for gas in the pit with a lighted match
    B. check pit cover joints with soap solution for seepage of gas and then remove pit cover
    C. remove pit cover and allow the pit to be ventilated
    D. remove pit cover and enter pit using a handkerchief as a mask to filter out any harmful gases

13. While a building owner is escorting an inspector to the cellar of the building, the building owner slips on the cellar stairs and falls and breaks his leg.
    Of the following types of first aid procedures, the one that is BEST for the inspector to take in this case is to

    A. move the victim to a warm place
    B. place the victim's leg in cold water to minimize swelling
    C. keep the victim still and try to keep him warm
    D. give the victim a stimulant to drink

14. An inspector finds that the sidewalk cellar door is open at a premises in which he is supposed to read the water meter.
Of the following, the BEST course of action for him to take is to

   A. enter the cellar and read the meter before anyone interferes
   B. obtain authorization from a responsible person at the premises before entering the cellar
   C. make some deliberate noise, by banging on the door, to determine if an unrestrained dog is on the premises and, if not, enter the cellar
   D. make an estimate of the meter reading to save the time and effort of searching through the cellar

15. While reading water meters at a premise, an inspector is confronted by the owner who asks him to clean out the clogged drain of a kitchen sink.
Of the following, the BEST course of action for the inspector to take is to

   A. comply with the request for a small fee, if it does not interfere with the day's assignment
   B. attempt the job for non-monetary compensation
   C. recommend the Roto-Rooter man
   D. politely refuse to comply with the request

16. The rules and regulations governing and restricting the use and supply of water allow authorized meter repair companies, with a meter repair permit, to make repairs on the premises of

   A. hot water meters, regardless of size but not cold water meters
   B. cold water meters, regardless of size, and hot water meters larger than three inches in size
   C. all meters less than three inches in size, hot or cold water
   D. only cold water meters, three inches in size and larger

17. According to the rules and regulations governing and restricting the use and supply of water, all water meter valves should be standard _____ valves.

   A. gate    B. globe    C. needle    D. angle

18. According to the rules and regulations governing and restricting the use and supply of water, the water which must be metered in the construction of an eight-story apartment building is

   A. only the water used in building the seventh and eighth stories
   B. all the water used in the construction of that building
   C. all the water used after the basement is constructed
   D. none at all, since the building is not a commercial establishment

19. According to the rules and regulations governing and restricting the use and supply of water, a meter pit must have an air vent if the meter pit contains a(n)

   A. meter by-pass            B. sewer trap
   C. airtight metal door      D. meter outlet valve

20. According to the rules and regulations governing and restricting the use and supply of water, on a 1" meter setting, the check valve shall be placed between the

   A. front wall and the service valve
   B. service valve and the meter
   C. meter and the test tee
   D. test tee and the outlet valve

20.____

21. The plumbing connection illustrated at the right is a(n)

   A. *correct* installation according to the building code
   B. *incorrect* installation because it is illegal for a drain to empty into a stack
   C. *incorrect* installation because each lavatory should enter into a separate stack
   D. *incorrect* installation because the two wastes should enter the stack at a higher elevation with respect to the trap

21.____

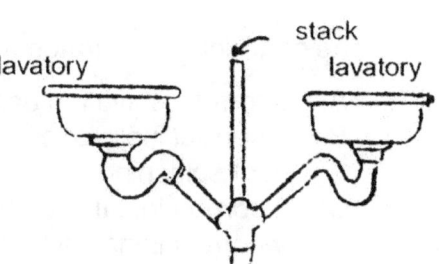

22.

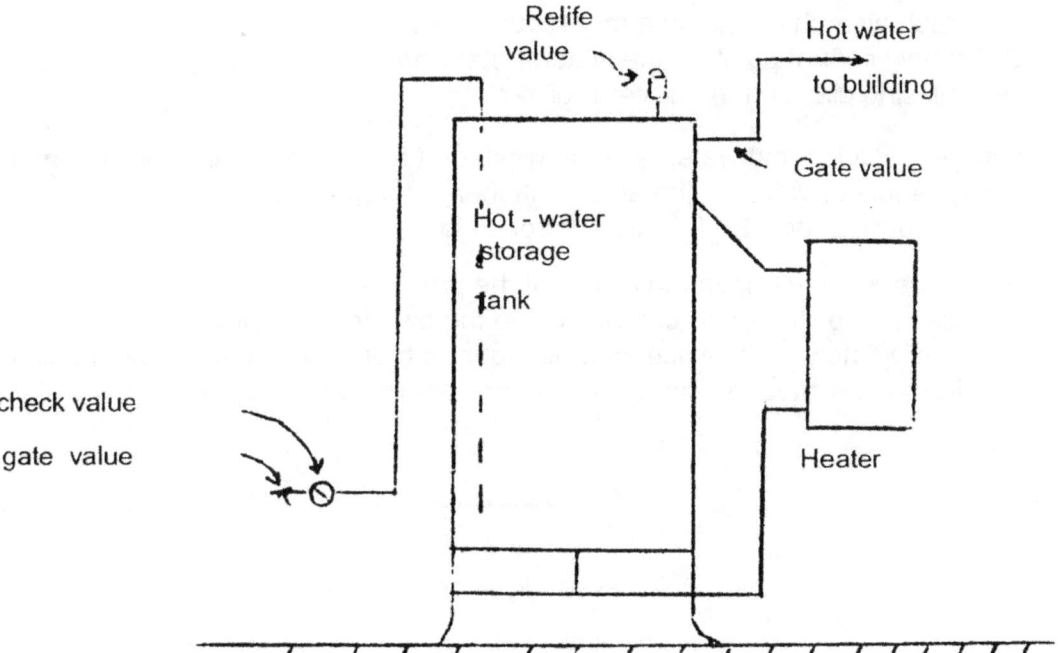

22.____

The plumbing connection illustrated on the previous page is a(n)

   A. *correct* installation according to the building code
   B. *incorrect* installation because the check valve should be located on the hot water line
   C. *incorrect* installation because the gate valves should be eliminated
   D. *incorrect* installation because the hot water storage tank should be vented to the atmosphere

23.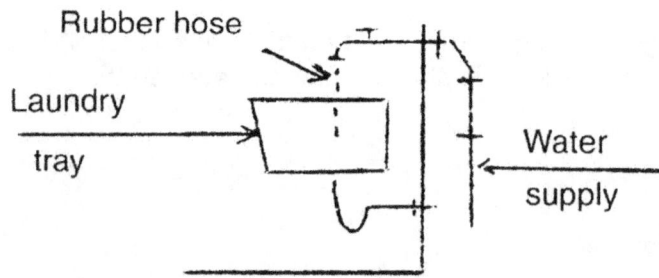

The connection illustrated above is a(n)
- A. *correct* installation according to the building code
- B. *incorrect* installation because the faucets should be located below the rim to prevent splashing
- C. *incorrect* installation because the hanging hose forms a potential cross connection
- D. *incorrect* installation because the hot water can enter the cold water pipe

24. Of the following, the indication that would cause the MOST suspicion that a water meter may have been illegally tampered with is
- A. a seal wire broken by corrosion
- B. fresh wrench marks on a meter outlet valve
- C. a new coat of paint on the water meter and surrounding pipes
- D. missing glass on the meter register

25. An inspector finds that water is being wasted at a commercial establishment because of a faulty regulator valve on the air conditioner at the premise.
Of the following, the BEST course of action for him to take is to
- A. issue a summons to the owner of the premise
- B. issue a notice of non-compliance to the owner of the premise
- C. immediately notify a licensed plumber so that he will make the necessary repair
- D. ignore the situation since all air conditioners use well water

## KEY (CORRECT ANSWERS)

1. A
2. B
3. B
4. B
5. C

6. C
7. B
8. B
9. B
10. B

11. B
12. C
13. C
14. B
15. D

16. D
17. A
18. B
19. B
20. D

21. D
22. A
23. C
24. D
25. B

---

# EXAMINATION SECTION
# TEST 1

DIRECTIONS: Each question or incomplete statement is followed by several suggested answers or completions. Select the one that BEST answers the question or completes the statement. *PRINT THE LETTER OF THE CORRECT ANSWER IN THE SPACE AT THE RIGHT.*

1. Of the following methods of installing pipe in a trench, the one which is MOST acceptable is to

    A. use a flat bottom trench and backfill not tamped
    B. have pipe supported on blocks and backfill tamped
    C. use a flat bottom trench and backfill tamped
    D. have pipe supported on blocks, backfill not tamped

    1.____

2. When cutting a 30" diameter cast iron pipe, it is BEST to use a(n)

    A. cold chisel
    B. diamond point chisel
    C. hardy
    D. ordinary wheel type of cutter

    2.____

3. Of the following materials, the one which is BEST suited for yarning bell and spigot joints on water pipe is

    A. plumber's yarn          B. boatmaker's yarn
    C. tar impregnated oakum   D. sterilized yarn

    3.____

4. A valve that is used between low pressure and high pressure areas in water distribution systems is called a boundary valve.

    A. pressure reducing       B. check
    C. gate                    D. globe

    4.____

5. Cast iron pipe is particularly adapted to underground and submerged service because of its

    A. ease in handling and joining
    B. high corrosion-resisting qualities
    C. ability to withstand high pressures
    D. low first cost

    5.____

6. In caulking a pipe joint, excessive *caulking* should be avoided to prevent

    A. *thinning* the lead     B. a second pouring of lead
    C. *misses*                D. bell damage

    6.____

7. The material used to disinfect water pipes before and after laying the pipe is USUALLY

    A. chlordane               B. calcium chloride
    C. chlorine                D. washing soda

    7.____

8. Of the following items, the one that is NOT a component part of a mechanical joint is a(n)

   A. yarn  B. gland
   C. rubber gasket  D. socket

9. Of the following causes of water leaks in mains, the one that is LEAST common is

   A. improper caulking
   B. poor backfilling
   C. improper handling of pipe
   D. manufacturing defects in the pipe

10. The BEST type of wrench to use for making up a mechanical joint in cast iron pipe is a _____ wrench.

    A. ratchet  B. monkey  C. strap  D. Stillson

11. The MAIN difference between skeleton sheathing and tight sheathing is that in skeleton sheathing

    A. a greater part of the sheathing is omitted
    B. reinforced laced type of sheathing is used
    C. the rangers and braces are placed differently
    D. no planks are used

12. The width of the trench at each caulking joint, in comparison with the remaining portion of the trench, should generally be

    A. equal to twice the diameter of the pipe to allow for caulking
    B. of sufficient size to allow for caulking
    C. equal to the diameter of the pipe plus 12 inches
    D. equal to the diameter of the pipe plus 1/2 pipe radius

13. Unless otherwise directed, a trench for a water pipe line should USUALLY be excavated to a depth of 4 feet measured from the surface of the roadway to the _____ of the pipe.

    A. center  B. bottom  C. invert  D. top

14. The length of trench excavation for the installation of a 30-inch pipe should NOT exceed _____ feet.

    A. 1500  B. 1300  C. 1100  D. 1000

15. Before laying a new water main, test pits or test trenches may be necessary in order to determine

    A. the amount of materials required
    B. subsurface obstructions
    C. the proper width of excavation
    D. the amount of labor needed

16. The outside circumference of a pipe that has an outside diameter of 11 1/2" is MOST NEARLY

    A. 32"  B. 36"  C. 39"  D. 42"

17. Continuous sheathing is USUALLY used when excavating a trench in

    A. unstable soil
    B. firm earth
    C. stiff clay
    D. rock

18. Assume that a pump is pumping water out of an excavated trench at the rate of 30 gallons per minute.
    The time that is required to pump 2700 gallons of water out of this trench would be MOST NEARLY _____ hour(s).

    A. 4 1/2
    B. 3
    C. 1 1/2
    D. 3/4

19. The size of *rangers* that should be used for trenches dug to a depth of seven (7) feet is APPROXIMATELY

    A. 1" x 2"
    B. 2" x 3"
    C. 2" x 4"
    D. 4" x 6"

20. The bottom of wood sheathing is USUALLY

    A. squared on all sides
    B. steel tipped in order to penetrate hard material
    C. capped in order to prevent splintering
    D. bevelled on both one face and one edge

21. The quickest and easiest way of disconnecting a bell and spigot lead joint in a pipe is by

    A. using a picking chisel at the joint
    B. cracking the bell
    C. melting the lead at the joint with an acetylene torch
    D. using a diamond point chisel

22. A joint runner is USUALLY used as a

    A. guide for molten lead
    B. scab on sheathing
    C. clamp for two pipes
    D. filler between pavement joints

23. Of the following tools, the one which is NOT usually used for caulking a joint is the

    A. stub
    B. regular
    C. cold chisel
    D. diamond joint

24. The type of lead USUALLY used to caulk cast iron pipe joints in water mains is

    A. lead wool
    B. shredded lead
    C. leadite
    D. pure soft lead

25. The distance that a *ranger* is USUALLY placed below the surface of a roadway is APPROXIMATELY

    A. 12"
    B. 10"
    C. 8"
    D. 6"

26. The proper manner to unload cast iron pipe at a trench site which is APPROXIMATELY 300 feet long is to

   A. stack it at convenient locations
   B. stack it in even layers with 4" x 4" stringers between each layer with blocks at each end
   C. lay it along the route with the bell facing in the direction in which the work is to proceed
   D. store it where it will not collect rain water and be damaged in freezing weather

27. Damage to cast iron pipe may sometimes result from rough handling when in transit. A simple method of determining whether the pipe was damaged or not is to

   A. *ring* each length with a hammer
   B. drop the pipe to see if it breaks
   C. hydraulically test the pipe
   D. visually examine the pipe for cracks

28. A blowoff connection in a water distribution main is USUALLY located at the

   A. highest point of the line
   B. lowest point of the line
   C. midway point between two distribution mains
   D. center line of the pipe

29. The proper depth of lead joints for a 4" or 6" cast iron pipe is MOST NEARLY _____ inches.

   A. 3 1/2   B. 3 1/4   C. 3   D. 2 3/8

30. The distance that fire hydrants should be located back from the face of the curb line is MOST NEARLY

   A. 6-10"   B. 12-16"   C. 18-20"   D. 22-26"

31. Your orders to your crew are MOST likely to be followed if you

   A. explain the reasons for these orders
   B. warn that all violators will be punished
   C. promise easy assignments to those who follow these orders best
   D. say that they are for the good of the department

32. In order to be a good supervisor, you should

   A. impress upon your men that you demand perfection in their work at all times
   B. avoid being blamed for your crew's mistakes
   C. impress your superior with your ability
   D. see to it that your men get what they are entitled to

33. In giving instructions to a crew, you should

   A. speak in as loud a tone as possible
   B. speak in a coaxing persuasive manner
   C. speak quietly, clearly, and courteously
   D. always use the word *please* when giving instructions

34. The BEST procedure to follow when a difficult and unusual problem arises involving the laying of a water pipe is to

    A. ask another pipe caulker for his opinion
    B. proceed working in the usual manner
    C. report the situation to the engineer
    D. continue working, making necessary changes yourself

35. Assume that you are in charge of a crew making repairs on a water main. A bystander whom you do not know begins to comment on the way the work is being done. He makes several suggestions which he claims will result in a better job.
    Of the following, you should

    A. hold up the work until you can discuss the suggestions with your superior
    B. listen to him, thank him, and proceed with the work as you have been doing
    C. tell him to go along about his own business since you can do the job without any advice
    D. tell him to take his comments and suggestions to your superior who has the authority to change procedure

36. Assume that a pipe worker earns $16,625 per year. If seventeen percent of his pay is deducted for taxes, social security, and pension, his net weekly pay will be APPROXIMATELY

    A. $319.70   B. $300.80   C. $290.60   D. $265.00

37. If eighteen (18) feet of 4" cast iron pipe weighs approximately 390 pounds, the weight of this pipe per lineal foot will be MOST NEARLY _____ lbs.

    A. 19   B. 21   C. 23   D. 25

38. A one-sixteenth cast iron fitting will change the direction of water APPROXIMATELY

    A. 90°   B. 45°   C. 22 1/2°   D. 11 1/4°

39. The overall length of a standard cast iron bell-and-spigot water pipe is MOST NEARLY

    A. 10' 4 1/2"   B. 11'9"   C. 12' 4 1/2"   D. 20'0"

40. In rock excavations, the minimum depth that rock must be removed from the bottom of the bell of a cast iron pipe to the bottom of a trench should be MOST NEARLY

    A. 3"   B. 4"   C. 6"   D. 9"

## KEY (CORRECT ANSWERS)

| | | | | | | | |
|---|---|---|---|---|---|---|---|
| 1. | C | 11. | A | 21. | C | 31. | A |
| 2. | B | 12. | B | 22. | A | 32. | D |
| 3. | D | 13. | D | 23. | D | 33. | C |
| 4. | C | 14. | D | 24. | D | 34. | C |
| 5. | B | 15. | B | 25. | A | 35. | B |
| 6. | D | 16. | B | 26. | C | 36. | D |
| 7. | C | 17. | A | 27. | A | 37. | B |
| 8. | A | 18. | C | 28. | B | 38. | C |
| 9. | D | 19. | D | 29. | D | 39. | C |
| 10. | A | 20. | D | 30. | C | 40. | C |

# TEST 2

DIRECTIONS: Each question or incomplete statement is followed by several suggested answers or completions. Select the one that BEST answers the question or completes the statement. *PRINT THE LETTER OF THE CORRECT ANSWER IN THE SPACE AT THE RIGHT.*

1. If four (4) men are *backfilling* a trench, the proper number of men for *tamping* should usually be NOT LESS than       1.____

    A. 2    B. 4    C. 6    D. 8

2. A subsurface leak in a street main may be located by means of a(n)       2.____

    A. amprobe
    B. aquaphone
    C. aqueduct
    D. drill rod

3. The FIRST step in shutting off a water main in a street is to       3.____

    A. close the blowoff and notify the Department of Public Works
    B. close the blowoff and notify the Police Department
    C. notify the householders and the Fire Department
    D. close the head gates and notify the Fire Department

4. Concentric reducers are used for       4.____

    A. maintaining the same center line elevation
    B. keeping the bottom of the pipe at the same level
    C. changing the direction of flow in a pipe
    D. lowering the inverts of the pipe

5. A valve box is generally built with an open bottom so that       5.____

    A. the valve box can rest directly on the pipe
    B. the valve can be removed rapidly
    C. any water seeping into it will drain away
    D. a bottom connection can be made

6. If lead that is being used for caulking is overheated, it will be found that the caulked lead ring from a joint would MOST likely be       6.____

    A. too soft    B. porous    C. brittle    D. flexible

7. A pipe compound used for making up threaded joints USUALLY acts as a filler between the threads and also as a       7.____

    A. hardener
    B. lubricant
    C. cleanser
    D. coolant

8. By referring to a concrete mix having a ratio of 1:2:4 is meant that the ingredients are made up of 1 part _____, 2 parts _____, and 4 parts _____.       8.____

    A. cement; sand; gravel
    B. sand; cement; water
    C. gravel; sand; cement
    D. sand; cement; gravel

9. The total weight of materials (lead and hemp) used in caulking an 8" bell and spigot joint for water is MOST NEARLY _____ lbs.

   A. 7   B. 10   C. 15   D. 24

10. Assume that a length of cast iron pipe measures 9'8" and three pieces of pipe are to be cut from this pipe, one 2'9", the second 3'2", and the third 1'10".
    The amount of pipe remaining after making these cuts (assuming no waste) is MOST NEARLY

    A. 1'6"   B. 1'9"   C. 1'11"   D. 2'2"

11. Of the following types of valves, the one that is used to permit the flow of water in one direction is the _____ valve.

    A. gate   B. angle   C. globe   D. check

12. Water mains in the city are generally located APPROXIMATELY _____ feet from the _____ line.

    A. four (4); curb
    B. five (5); sewer
    C. six (6); building
    D. nine (9); curb

13. Of the following equipment, the one which a pipe worker is NOT normally required to know how to operate is the

    A. backhoe
    B. air-powered chipping hammers and caulking tools
    C. various types of pipe laying derricks
    D. air-powered pavement breakers and rock drills

14. Assume that, after installing a mechanical joint in a water main, a leak occurs around the joint.
    Of the following, the BEST practice to follow would be to

    A. retighten the bolts
    B. loosen the bolts to expand the rubber gasket
    C. *hammer* home the spigot into the bell
    D. disassemble the joint, clean thoroughly, and reassemble

15. It is a good policy to keep excavated material away from the edge of a trench a distance of AT LEAST

    A. 2 feet   B. 18 inches   C. 1 foot   D. 6 inches

16. Neglecting friction, the height, in feet, to which water can rise having a pressure of 55 pounds per square inch is MOST NEARLY

    A. 120   B. 150   C. 180   D. 210

17. If it takes 3 men 11 days to dig a trench, the number of days it will take 5 men to dig the same trench, assuming all work is done at the same rate of speed, is MOST NEARLY

    A. 6 1/2   B. 7 3/4   C. 8 1/4   D. 8 3/4

18. It is sometimes found that poured lead joints tend to crack open due to shrinkage. This is USUALLY due to

    A. overheating of the lead
    B. impurities in the lead
    C. excessive pressure at the joint
    D. cooling of the lead

19. The BEST material to use for backfilling trenches that are made in rock is USUALLY

    A. tan bark    B. cinders    C. gravel    D. sand

20. For an average pipe repair job, it is the practice to use a gang made up of

    A. one pipe caulker and three laborers
    B. two pipe caulkers and three laborers
    C. one supervisor, two pipe caulkers, and two laborers
    D. three laborers and two helpers

21. Slack in cables or tie rods is USUALLY *taken up* by the use of

    A. drift pins           B. clamps
    C. Crosby clips         D. turnbuckles

22. A pneumatic tool is one that is USUALLY directly operated by means of

    A. gasoline             B. compressed air
    C. oil pressure         D. electricity

23. The BEST thing to do when a pavement breaker becomes jammed in the pavement is to

    A. attempt to work it loose without using another breaker
    B. shut off the air compressor
    C. increase the air supply
    D. use another pavement breaker to cut it loose

24. If a trench is dug 6'0" deep, 2'6" wide, and 8'0" long, the area of the opening, in square feet, is MOST NEARLY

    A. 48    B. 32    C. 20    D. 15

Questions 25-30.

DIRECTIONS: Questions 25 through 30 are to be answered in accordance with the sketch shown on the following page, which represents a portion of a water distribution map and other facilities.

4 (#2)

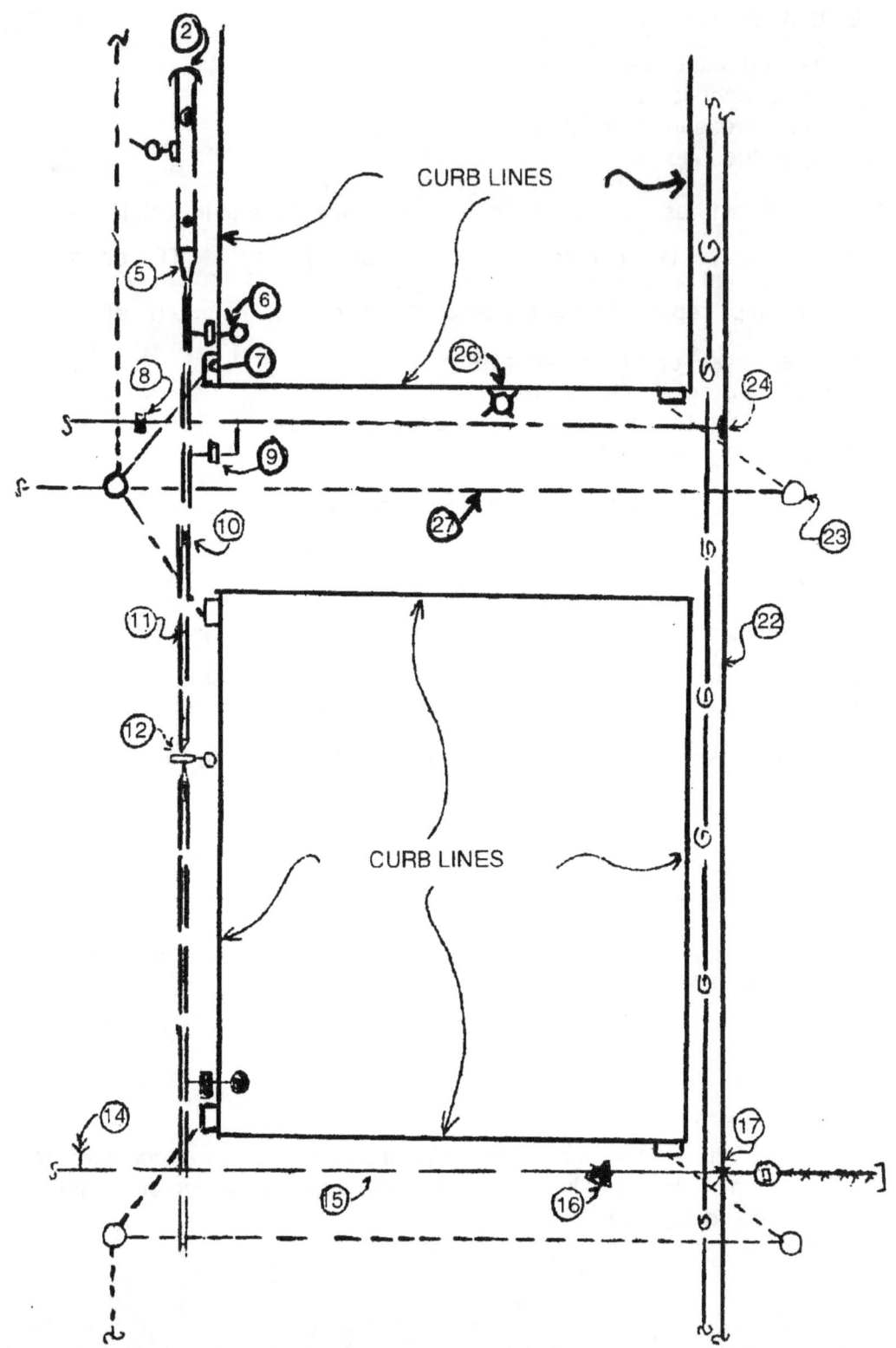

The above sketch represents a portion of a water distribution map and other facilities. To be used in answering questions numbered 25 to 30 inclusive.

25. A hydrant symbol is numbered

    A. 26  B. 14  C. 6  D. 9

26. A cap symbol is numbered

    A. 2  B. 5  C. 9  D. 10

27. Of the following numbered lines, the one which is NOT a water line is numbered

    A. 11  B. 15  C. 22  D. 27

28. A reducer symbol is numbered

    A. 8  B. 16  C. 12  D. 14

29. A catch basin symbol is numbered

    A. 7  B. 10  C. 23  D. 24

30. A valve symbol is numbered

    A. 17  B. 14  C. 10  D. 8

31. Opening a fire hydrant near the high point of a newly installed portion of a water main, prior to testing, is USUALLY done in order to remove

    A. air
    B. obstructions
    C. slime growths
    D. P. mineral deposits

32. Taps, or wet connections to a city main, may be made by

    A. a licensed plumber
    B. the Department of Water Supply, Gas and Electricity
    C. the Department of Public Works
    D. any experienced laborer

33. The supervisor made a ridiculous statement. As used in this sentence, the word ridiculous means MOST NEARLY

    A. incorrect  B. evil  C. unfriendly  D. foolish

34. That pipe caulker is engaged in a hazardous job. As used in this sentence, the word hazardous means MOST NEARLY

    A. inconvenient
    B. dangerous
    C. difficult
    D. demanding

35. Breaks in water distribution mains are front page news for the very reason that they occur infrequently. As used in this sentence, the word infrequently means MOST NEARLY

    A. at regular intervals
    B. often
    C. rarely
    D. unexpectedly

36. Several kinds of self-caulking substitutes for lead have been developed. As used in this sentence, the word substitutes means MOST NEARLY

    A. additives
    B. replacements
    C. hardeners
    D. softeners

37. Cast iron is essentially an alloy of iron and carbon. As used in this sentence, the word essentially means MOST NEARLY

   A. never   B. basically   C. barely   D. sometimes

38. A pipe worker sometimes makes a trivial mistake. As used in this sentence, the word trivial means MOST NEARLY

   A. common
   C. obvious
   B. significant
   D. unimportant

39. When water moves through pipe, friction is developed between the water and the inside surface of the pipe. As used in this sentence, the word friction means MOST NEARLY

   A. resistance
   C. slippage
   B. heat
   D. pressure

40. Assume that a piece of cast iron pipe has to be cut to fit between two cast iron bells fixed in place in a trench. Of the following statements, the one which is MOST NEARLY correct is that, if the pipe is cut too

   A. short, the next joint may have to be broken to make up the difference
   B. short, the yarn used for caulking might be pushed through past the end of the pipe
   C. long, the proper amount of caulking lead could not be used at the joints
   D. long, the joint would need a bottom support

## KEY (CORRECT ANSWERS)

| | | | |
|---|---|---|---|
| 1. B | 11. D | 21. D | 31. A |
| 2. B | 12. D | 22. B | 32. B |
| 3. C | 13. A | 23. D | 33. D |
| 4. A | 14. D | 24. C | 34. B |
| 5. C | 15. A | 25. C | 35. C |
| 6. C | 16. A | 26. A | 36. B |
| 7. B | 17. A | 27. D | 37. B |
| 8. A | 18. D | 28. B | 38. D |
| 9. C | 19. D | 29. A | 39. A |
| 10. C | 20. A | 30. D | 40. B |

# EXAMINATION SECTION
# TEST 1

DIRECTIONS: Each question or incomplete statement is followed by several suggested answers or completions. Select the one that BEST answers the question or completes the statement. *PRINT THE LETTER OF THE CORRECT ANSWER IN THE SPACE AT THE RIGHT.*

1. The seal of a trap is made of

    A. a bronze gate  
    B. a bronze ball  
    C. water  
    D. air

2. When a plumber is using a turnpin, he SHOULD be

    A. removing kinks from a lead bend
    B. cleaning a lead joint for wiping
    C. straightening out a piece of lead pipe
    D. flaring the end of a lead pipe

3. A water meter measures and registers water consumption in

    A. gallons per minute  
    B. cubic feet per hour  
    C. quarts per second  
    D. cubic feet

4. The part that is connected to a ballcock that insures a full trap seal is the

    A. float ball  
    B. upper liftrod  
    C. hush tube  
    D. refill tube

5. PROPER protection against excessive pressure within a hot water storage tank is provided by installing a _____ valve.

    A. pressure relief  
    B. check  
    C. flow  
    D. gate

6. A one-sixteenth bend is EQUIVALENT to a fitting having an angle of _____ degrees.

    A. 22 1/2    B. 30    C. 45    D. 60

7. A 3-inch standard weight water pipe and a 3-inch extra heavy water pipe have the SAME

    A. I.D.  
    B. O.D.  
    C. wall thickness  
    D. weight per foot

8. Of the following materials, the one that is NOT used in caulking a cast iron bell and spigot water pipe joint is

    A. asbestos rope  
    B. oakum rope  
    C. treated paper rope  
    D. molded rings

9. The reason a cast iron hub is hit before joining the hub with a spigot is to determine its

    A. soundness  
    B. weight  
    C. wall thickness  
    D. material content

10. The inside diameter of a 4" brass caulking ferrule is MOST NEARLY

   A. 3 7/8"   B. 4"   C. 4 1/8"   D. 4 1/4"

11. Cast brass floor flanges used for water closets should have a MINIMUM thickness of

   A. 1/2"   B. 3/8"   C. 1/4"   D. 1/8"

12. The trap of a water closet is located

   A. in the water closet
   B. in the lead bend
   C. under the water closet
   D. in the soil stack

13. Of the following, a PROPER reason why a plumber should install a check valve is to

   A. relieve pressure in the storage tank
   B. prevent a backflow of sewer gas
   C. allow a flow of water in one direction only
   D. reduce the volume of water in an appliance

14. The PURPOSE of an air chamber in a water line is to

   A. allow for expansion of water
   B. increase water pressure in the riser
   C. reduce water hammer in the system
   D. decrease velocity of the flow of water

15. As used by a plumber, a leader is a

   A. section of a soil stack
   B. vertical storm water pipe line
   C. part of a bath waste
   D. part of a croton

16. The bib-screw in a faucet retains the

   A. seat
   B. handle
   C. washer
   D. packing nut

17. When testing for leaks in gas lines, it is BEST to use

   A. water in the lines under pressure
   B. a lighted candle
   C. an aquastat
   D. soapy water

18. Drain lines receiving the discharge from chemistry laboratory sinks should be made of

   A. galvanized steel
   B. duriron or pyrex
   C. cast iron
   D. brass or copper

19. Of the following, the one that is BEST to use when testing for leaks in a new gas pipe installation is a

   A. geiger counter
   B. vacuum gauge
   C. mercury column
   D. water column

20. A plumber should know that installing a globe valve on a cold water line will cut down the _____ of the water.

    A. volume
    B. temperature
    C. viscosity
    D. resistance

21. Of the following tools, the one which is NOT used when working a wiped joint is the

    A. drift plug
    B. bending iron
    C. reamer
    D. turnpin

22. The amount of lead to be used to complete a caulked cast iron soil joint should NOT be less than _____ of the diameter of the pipe.

    A. 10 ounces for each inch
    B. 12 ounces for each inch
    C. 14 ounces for each inch
    D. one full medium-sized ladle regardless

23. A shave hook is recommended by its manufacturer for

    A. evening the edges of lead
    B. brightening oxidized copper
    C. removing burrs from non-ferrous pipe
    D. removing oxidation from lead

24. The MAIN purpose of a house trap is to

    A. provide the house drain with a cleanout
    B. prevent gases from the public sewer from entering the house plumbing system
    C. *trap* articles of value that are lost
    D. eliminate the necessity for traps under all other fixtures

25. A corporation cock or stop is a

    A. self-closing faucet
    B. shut-off valve for a lavoratory
    C. frost-proof type of hydrant
    D. shut-off valve for a water service

26. A 45-degree offset included in a house drain should contain ONLY

    A. one 1/4 bend and one 1/16 bend
    B. one 1/4 bend and one 1/8 bend
    C. two 1/8 bends
    D. two 1/4 bends

27. A plumber prevents siphonage in a fixture trap if he

    A. vents properly
    B. installs a relief valve
    C. installs the correct number of check valves
    D. provides adequate pitch on the water lines

28. A 28 ft. long pipe line, stalled with a pitch of 1/4 inch per foot, has a TOTAL fall of _____ inches.

   A. 3 1/4   B. 7   C. 10 1/2   D. 14

29. The length of a pipe measuring 37.875 inches, end-to-end, is EQUAL to 3 ft. + _____ inches.

   A. 0 7/8   B. 1 1/4   C. 1 5/8   D. 1 7/8

30. A waste stack may receive the discharge from _____ water closet(s).

   A. no
   B. only one
   C. two
   D. three or more

31. Capillary action is used in the CORRECT joining of _____ joints.

   A. bell and spigot
   B. screw-pipe
   C. copper-tube sweat
   D. lead-wiped

32. The TOTAL length of four pieces of 1 1/2" galvanized steel pipe whose lengths are 7 ft. + 3 1/2 inches, 4 ft. + 2 1/4 inches, 6 ft. + 7 inches, and 8 ft. + 5 1/8 inches, is _____ ft. + _____ inches.

   A. 26; 5 7/8
   B. 25; 6 7/8
   C. 25; 4 1/4
   D. 25; 3 3/8

33. To a plumber, the letters I.P.S. mean

   A. internal pipe size
   B. iron pipe size
   C. interior pressure standards
   D. international pipe standard.

34. Of the following, the tool that SHOULD be used on polished pipe surface is the

   A. Stillson wrench
   B. strap wrench
   C. chain tongs
   D. crescent wrench

35. In plumbing, the abbreviation X.H.C.I. is associated with

   A. water heaters
   B. chemical waste lines
   C. air lines
   D. house drains

36. A yarning iron SHOULD be used in

   A. tinning copper fittings
   B. making lead safes
   C. making bell and spigot joints
   D. drying a water-filled trench

37. If a 45-degree offset is 12 inches in length, the length of its diagonal or travel is _____ inches.

   A. 17   B. 18   C. 19   D. 20

38. *Plumbers Soil* is GENERALLY used by plumbers as an aid in  38.____

    A. wiping lead joints
    B. making up flange joints
    C. backfilling a trench
    D. threading steel pipes

39. Of the following types of saws, the one that SHOULD be used for cutting lead pipe is the _____ saw.  39.____

    A. cross-cut
    B. rip
    C. hack
    D. dove-tail

40. Of the following fixtures, the one that plumbers USUALLY call the *unit fixture* is the  40.____

    A. water closet
    B. slop sink
    C. lavatory
    D. bathtub

---

## KEY (CORRECT ANSWERS)

| | | | | | | | |
|---|---|---|---|---|---|---|---|
| 1. | C | 11. | D | 21. | C | 31. | C |
| 2. | D | 12. | A | 22. | B | 32. | A |
| 3. | D | 13. | C | 23. | D | 33. | B |
| 4. | D | 14. | C | 24. | B | 34. | B |
| 5. | A | 15. | B | 25. | D | 35. | D |
| 6. | A | 16. | C | 26. | C | 36. | C |
| 7. | B | 17. | D | 27. | A | 37. | A |
| 8. | B | 18. | B | 28. | B | 38. | A |
| 9. | A | 19. | C | 29. | D | 39. | A |
| 10. | D | 20. | A | 30. | A | 40. | C |

# TEST 2

DIRECTIONS: Each question or incomplete statement is followed by several suggested answers or completions. Select the one that BEST answers the question or completes the statement. *PRINT THE LETTER OF THE CORRECT ANSWER IN THE SPACE AT THE RIGHT.*

1. The vertical distance between the crown weir and the dip of a trap is called the
   A. jumpover
   B. air gap
   C. seal depth
   D. diameter of the trap

2. Of the following, the composition of general purpose *wiping solder* is _____ tin and _____ lead.
   A. 70%; 30%   B. 60%; 40%   C. 50%; 50%   D. 35%; 65%

3. Of the following wrenches, the one which should be used on screwed valves and fittings having hexagonal connections is the _____ wrench.
   A. pipe   B. monkey   C. chuck   D. strap

4. A cast iron coupling that has one end threaded for screw pipe and the other end hubbed to receive the spigot end of a pipe is known as a(n)
   A. sisson fitting
   B. tucker fitting
   C. union
   D. F & W fitting

5. The size of a fresh-air inlet is based on the size of the associated
   A. house drain
   B. public sewer
   C. house sewer
   D. soil stack

6. The tool that holds the dies when pipe is being threaded is called a
   A. yoke   B. vise   C. stock   D. swedge

7. A gallon of water weighs MOST NEARLY _____ lbs.
   A. 6.25   B. 7.5   C. 8.33   D. 14.7

8. A *solder nipple* is MAINLY used in plumbing work to
   A. maintain an even flow of solder
   B. connect the handle of a soldering iron to the *copper*
   C. make up a joint between lead pipe and brass pipe
   D. clean clogged pipes

9. Where steel hangers are used to support copper pipe, the pipe should be insulated from the hangers to prevent
   A. water hammer
   B. vibration
   C. cooling
   D. electrolysis

10. Copper tubing having the GREATEST wall thickness is known as _____ copper tubing.
    A. D.W.V. type
    B. type M
    C. type L
    D. type K

11. Of the following methods, the BEST one to use in making up a pipe joint between lead pipe and copper pipe is

    A. brazing
    B. soldering
    C. burning
    D. wiping

12. To *break in* or condition a new asbestos joint runner, the runner SHOULD be soaked in

    A. alcohol   B. rosin   C. oil   D. water

13. The weight of a 4 ft. x 4 ft. shower pan made of 6-pound lead is MOST NEARLY _____ pounds.

    A. 96   B. 75   C. 69   D. 29.25

14. The approved method of making a branch connection to an existing horizontal cast iron wasteline is by using a

    A. sisson fitting
    B. kaeffer fitting
    C. saddle
    D. three-piece connection

15. A *hydropneumatic* tank in a plumbing system is MAINLY used to

    A. pump storm water to the sewer
    B. provide potable water under pressure
    C. supply compressed air to equipment
    D. filter water for a swimming pool.

16. Syphon action through the fill pipe in a flush tank is prevented by installing a

    A. stop and waste valve
    B. vacuum breaker
    C. flushometer
    D. back-water valve

17. Sperm candle or tallon is applied to clean lead work in order to PREVENT

    A. pitting
    B. oxidation
    C. tinning
    D. melting

18. Joints for cast iron bell and spigot soil pipe SHOULD be made with

    A. wiped solder
    B. packed oakum and molten lead
    C. oakum and asphaltic compound
    D. oakum and cement mortar

19. A tee whose branch is larger than the run is CORRECTLY referred to as a _____ tee.

    A. bullhead   B. lateral   C. street   D. reducing

20. A house drain which is buried in earth SHOULD be made of

    A. galvanized wrought iron
    B. galvanized steel
    C. transite
    D. uncoated cast iron

21. A compression type fitting is MOST frequently used with

    A. copper tubing
    B. steel pipe
    C. transite
    D. cast iron pipe

22. Safety goggles should be worn when cutting

    A. galvanized pipe
    B. oakum
    C. cast iron
    D. sheet lead

23. A plumber should NOT plunge a wet ladle into a pot of molten caulking lead because it

    A. contaminates the lead
    B. may crack the pot
    C. may crack the ladle
    D. makes the lead spatter

24. A plumber's helper who is careless is one who is

    A. negligent
    B. untrained
    C. neat
    D. methodical

25. A CORRECTLY installed gasket provides a seal in a

    A. flange union
    B. ground joint union
    C. roof flange
    D. left-right coupling

26. A plumber installing a battery of sinks in the kitchen of a school cafeteria should also include in the waste line a(n)

    A. chlorinator
    B. anti-syphon loop
    C. grease trap
    D. check valve

27. If a faucet continues to drip despite the new washer a helper has installed, he SHOULD then

    A. reface or replace the seat
    B. install a washer made of different material
    C. replace the entire faucet
    D. replace the bib-screw

28. Of the following tools, the one used to fasten faucets to lavatories is called a(n)

    A. pair of pump pliers
    B. spud wrench
    C. open-end wrench
    D. basin wrench

29. A cast iron floor flange SHOULD be used when installing a

    A. water closet
    B. bathtub
    C. kitchen sink
    D. drinking fountain

30. A plumber's rasp is a tool recommended by its manufacturer for use on

    A. cast iron
    B. brass
    C. lead
    D. black steel

31. Of the following, the pipe size NOT common to the plumbing trade is _____ inch.

    A. 2
    B. 2 1/2
    C. 3
    D. 3 1/2

32. Once a flushometer valve is in operation, it is made to close automatically by the

    A. return of the lever handle to the neutral position
    B. action of a flat helical spring above the diaphragm
    C. water pressure on the inlet side of the valve
    D. elasticity of a stainless steel diaphragm

Questions 33-36.

DIRECTIONS: Questions 33 through 36, inclusive, are to be answered by referring to the following sketch of a piping arrangement.

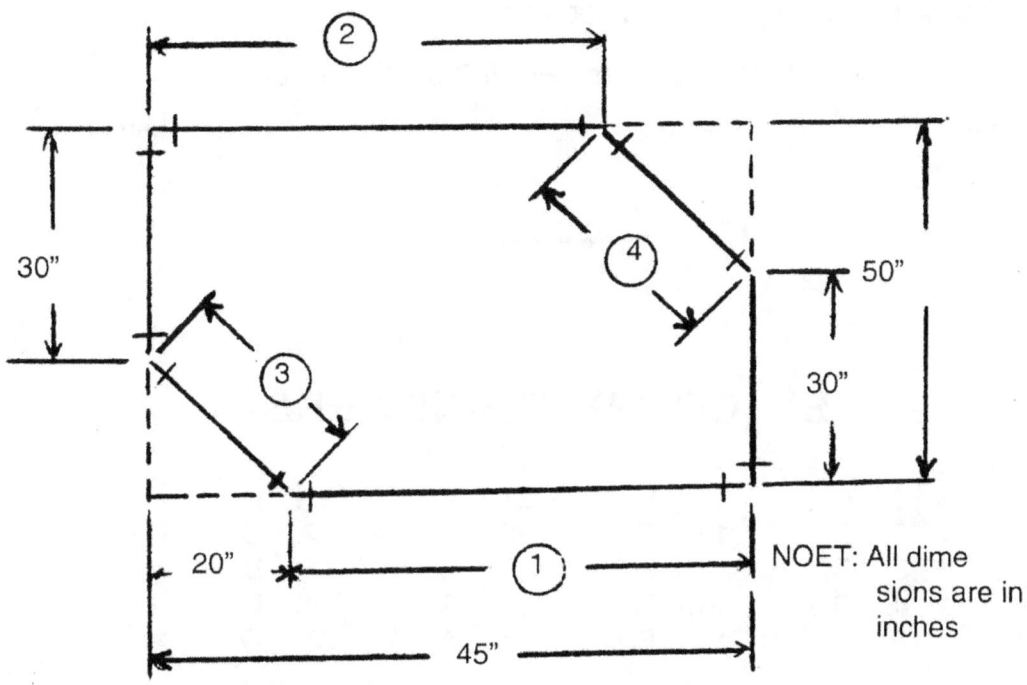

NOET: All dimesions are in inches

33. The center-to-center pipe measurement of *1* is MOST NEARLY equal to _____ inches.   33.____
    A. 20        B. 25        C. 30        D. 65

34. The center-to-center pipe measurement of *2* is MOST NEARLY equal to _____ inches.   34.____
    A. 20        B. 25        C. 30        D. 45

35. The center-to-center pipe measurement of *3* is MOST NEARLY equal to _____ inches.   35.____
    A. 30 1/2    B. 28 7/8    C. 28 1/4    D. 27 3/4

36. The center-to-center pipe measurement of *4* is MOST NEARLY equal to _____ inches.   36.____
    A. 23 1/2    B. 28 1/4    C. 29        D. 31 1/4

37. An outside caulking iron is a tool recommended by its manufacturer for use on   37.____
    A. steel pipe            B. cast iron
    C. lead pipe            D. brass pipe

38. A swimming pool is 25 feet wide by 75 feet long and has an average depth of 5 feet.   38.____
    The capacity when filled to the overflow is _____ gallons.
    A. 9,375     B. 65,625    C. 69,005    D. 70,312

39. A tap borer SHOULD be used by a plumber when 39.____
    A. cutting internal threads
    B. preparing copper joints for sweating
    C. joining cast iron to screw pipe
    D. preparing soil lead pipe for a solder nipple

40. A hydrostatic test on a plumbing system SHOULD be done by using 40.____
    A. water    B. smoke    C. air    D. kerosene

---

# KEY (CORRECT ANSWERS)

| | | | |
|---|---|---|---|
| 1. C | 11. D | 21. A | 31. D |
| 2. D | 12. C | 22. C | 32. C |
| 3. B | 13. A | 23. D | 33. B |
| 4. B | 14. D | 24. A | 34. B |
| 5. A | 15. B | 25. A | 35. C |
| 6. C | 16. B | 26. C | 36. B |
| 7. C | 17. B | 27. A | 37. B |
| 8. C | 18. B | 28. D | 38. D |
| 9. D | 19. A | 29. A | 39. D |
| 10. D | 20. D | 30. C | 40. A |

---

# EXAMINATION SECTION
# TEST 1

DIRECTIONS: Each question or incomplete statement is followed by several suggested answers or completions. Select the one that BEST answers the question or completes the statement. *PRINT THE LETTER OF THE CORRECT ANSWER IN THE SPACE AT THE RIGHT.*

1. The MAIN advantage of a rotary pump over a centrifugal pump is that it
    A. has more velocity
    B. has greater speed
    C. delivers more gallons per minute
    D. is self-priming and requires no valves

2. Pump efficiency can be termed
    I. hydraulic    II. volumetric    III. thermal    IV. mechanical

    The CORRECT answer is:
    A. I, II    B. I, III, IV    C. I, II, IV    D. I, II, III, IV

3. A superheater vent valve is installed on a boiler to
    A. insure a flow of steam through the superheater when steam is being raised on the boiler
    B. insure that some of the excess steam is released
    C. lower the steam temperature
    D. none of the above

4. Which of the following is a wearing ring on a centrifugal pump?
    A. Lantern    B. Turbine    C. Impeller    D. Thrust

5. Worn sealing rings can cause the
    A. capacity to increase
    B. discharge to flow back into the inlet
    C. priming to stop
    D. shaft to throw out of alignment

6. Vibration is caused by
    A. packing too tight         B. water hammer
    C. shaft alignment           D. worn bearings

7. A condensate pump helps to
    A. create vacuum in the system
    B. induce the steam to circulate rapidly
    C. return the condensate back to the boiler
    D. reduce the back pressure on the engine

8. Important pumps on a feedwater line are the
    I. rotary    II. vacuum    III. turbine    IV. centrifugal
    The CORRECT answer is:
    A. I, II    B. II, III, IV    C. I, II, III    D. I, II, III, IV

9. Which of the following is a reciprocating pump?
   A. Two stage
   B. Turbine
   C. Simplex
   D. All of the above

10. Which cylinder is larger on a duplex pump?
    A. Water
    B. Air
    C. Steam
    D. All are the same size

11. The FEWEST number of valves on a duplex pump is
    A. 4    B. 8    C. 12    D. 16

12. A pump may fail to discharge when the
    A. pump is not properly primed
    B. inlet valve is stuck
    C. valve seats are in bad condition
    D. all of the above

13. A pump may pound and vibrate because of
    A. air in the liquid
    B. a leaky inlet line
    C. excessive speed
    D. all of the above

14. If a pump races while increasing its output, the cause may be
    A. a leaky plunger
    B. a broken or stuck water valve
    C. an air leak
    D. not enough steam to move the piston

15. If the piston strikes the head of the cylinder, the cause would MOST probably be
    A. improper adjustment of the cushion valve
    B. cylinder rings are worn
    C. too much lap on the valves
    D. none of the above

16. To adjust the cushion valve, you should
    A. run the pump at full speed
    B. cut down the steam supply
    C. run the pump with a full load
    D. run the pump without a water load

17. If the pump lacks a cushion valve, you should
    A. lower the steam pressure
    B. adjust the lost motion enough to permit the pump to make a full stroke without striking
    C. adjust the piston rings
    D. adjust the back pressure valve

18. What condition would cause a piston to stop on dead center?
    A. The slide valve is worn
    B. There is not enough steam pressure
    C. There is too high of a head
    D. The cylinder shoulders are worn

19. Positive suction head is a condition present when the
    A. pump is located below the liquid supply
    B. pump is located between the boiler and the feedwater tank
    C. pump is located above the liquid supply
    D. water pressure is greater than the suction pressure

20. A centrifugal pump will most likely fail if
    A. the suction side of the pump is defective
    B. the discharge valve is closed
    C. wearing rings are worn
    D. strainer is clogged

21. The pump may fail to discharge if there is
    A. not enough water pressure
    B. improper priming
    C. air trapped at the top of the casing causing the pump to lose its discharge
    D. too high of a head

22. The failure of a pump to discharge can be rectified by
    A. increasing the water pressure
    B. reducing the pipe size
    C. decreasing the water pressure
    D. repriming the pump

23. To prevent a pump from failing to discharge, you should
    A. install a lantern ring
    B. replace the impeller
    C. install a bigger motor
    D. remove some packing

24. Reduction in both capacity and head is caused by
    A. too much air leaking through the packing
    B. reverse rotation of the motor
    C. a closed suction valve
    D. a clogged strainer

25. Small by-pass lines are installed around a large gate valve in order to
    A. equalize the pressure on the globe valve
    B. balance the pressure on the gate valve when the valve is being opened
    C. increase the velocity of the steam
    D. eliminate the sudden change in temperature of the steam

## KEY (CORRECT ANSWERS)

| | | |
|---|---|---|
| 1. D | | 11. B |
| 2. D | | 12. D |
| 3. A | | 13. D |
| 4. C | | 14. D |
| 5. B | | 15. A |
| 6. D | | 16. D |
| 7. C | | 17. B |
| 8. D | | 18. A |
| 9. C | | 19. A |
| 10. C | | 20. A |

21. B
22. D
23. A
24. B
25. B

# TEST 2

DIRECTIONS: Each question or incomplete statement is followed by several suggested answers or completions. Select the one that BEST answers the question or completes the statement. *PRINT THE LETTER OF THE CORRECT ANSWER IN THE SPACE AT THE RIGHT.*

1. The purpose of a volume casing on a centrifugal pump is to  1.\_\_\_\_\_
    A. convert velocity into vacuum
    B. convert velocity into pressure
    C. prevent cavitation of the pump
    D. increase the velocity of the water

2. How many type of feedwater heaters are currently in existence  2.\_\_\_\_\_
    A. 1  B. 2  C. 4  D. 5

3. Which of the following are types of feedwater heaters?  3.\_\_\_\_\_
    A. Economizer  B. Closed  C. Deaerator  D. All of the above

4. When the temperature leaving the feedwater heater is too low, the MAIN problem is probably that  4.\_\_\_\_\_
    A. steam pressure is too low
    B. back pressure is too low
    C. steam is of poor quality
    D. too much condensate is in the steam

5. The advantage of a feedwater heater is:  5.\_\_\_\_\_
    A. Hotter feedwater
    B. Less fuel consumption
    C. Less air in the feedwater
    D. All of the above

6. To increase the back pressure, you should  6.\_\_\_\_\_
    A. install a bigger back pressure valve
    B. put a heavier spring on the valve
    C. close the back pressure valve
    D. increase the line pressure

7. Which of the following is NOT a use of a feedwater heater? To  7.\_\_\_\_\_
    A. pre-heat the feedwater
    B. eliminate scale foaming substances by precipitation
    C. utilize some of the steam going to waste
    D. store generated steam

8. In relation to the feedwater pump, the feedwater heater should be located in another part of the building  8.\_\_\_\_\_
    A. in the basement of the plant
    B. about 10 or 12 feet above the pump

9. An open feedwater heater is a heater
   A. open at one end
   B. with steam coils
   C. where water and steam are in actual contact
   D. with 2/3 steam space

10. The MAIN advantage of an open heater is that it
    A. can separate scale forming substances from the feed-water by precipitation
    B. produces hotter water
    C. can hold more steam
    D. is cheap to operate

11. How much steam supply is sufficient for an open heater?
    A. 3 to 5 lbs.    B. 5 to 7 lbs.    C. 8 to 10 lbs.    D. All of the above

12. _____ A(n)    should be installed on an open feedwater heater
    A. exhaust or vent pipe          B. oil separator
    C. steam gauge                    D. all of the above

13. A closed feedwater heater is a heater in which
    A. steam travels through coils or tubes and water on the outside of the coils
    B. water runs through a tube with steam on the outside heating the water
    C. feedwater is heated and passed back to the deaerator
    D. none of the above

14. At what pressure should a feedwater heater operate?
    A. 1-15 lbs.    B. 15-20 lbs.    C. 20-25 lbs.    D. 25-30 lbs.

15. The safety device normally installed on a feedwater heater is a _____ valve.
    A. pneumatic                      B. pressure relief
    C. safety                         D. by-pass

16. The FIRST indication of a broken coil on a feedwater heater would be the
    A. heater filling up with water
    B. relief valve opening
    C. steam pressure increasing
    D. water pressure rising

17. On a double-acting reciprocating pump, what is installed on the discharge side of the pump? A(n)
    A. air chamber and gauge
    B. pressure gauge and relief valve.
    C. pressure gauge and safety valve
    D. air chamber and a gate valve

18. What types of lubricators are MOST commonly used today?
    I. Hydrokinetic            II. Force feed pump
    III. Splash system         IV. Gravity

    The CORRECT answer is:
    A. I, II          B. II, III, IV         C. I, III, IV         D. I, II, III, IV

19. What type of lubricant is used on piston rods and valve stems on a reciprocating pump?   19._____
    Mineral oil
    A. Compress oil
    B. Oil with high velocity
    C. Cylinder oil and graphite mixed together
    D. A reciprocating pump contains the following notation:

20. What is the diameter of the liquid cylinder? 7 x 6 x 4.   20._____
    A. 6"                           B. 4"
    C. 7"                           D. none of the above

21. What types of pumps are used in a heating system?   21._____
    I. Reciprocating               II. Condensate
    III. Centrifugal               IV. Vacuum

    The CORRECT answer is:
    A. I, II                        B. I, III
    C. II, IV                       D. III, IV

22. The purpose of a steam loop, or thermal pump, is to   22._____
    A. deliver steam to the engine
    B. protect water from entering the steam gauge
    C. return condensate back to the boiler
    D. trap steam from high pressure lines into a low-pressure line

23. What effect does a short stroke have on a reciprocating pump? It   23._____
    A. increases the pump capacity
    B. increases the steam capacity, and decreases the pump consumption
    C. increases the steam Consumption, and decreases the pump capacity
    D. relieves the pressure in the air chamber

24. A pump with two liquid cylinders, and one steam cylinder is called a   pump.   24._____
    A. triplex                      B. duplex
    C. tandem                       D. double tandem

25. The air chamber on a reciprocating pump is located on the   25._____
    A. discharge side of the feed pump
    B. discharge side of the reciprocating pump
    C. discharge side of all pumps
    D. suction side of a reciprocating pump

## KEY (CORRECT ANSWERS)

| | |
|---|---|
| 1. A | 11. D |
| 2. B | 12. D |
| 3. D | 13. A |
| 4. B | 14. A |
| 5. D | 15. B |
| 6. C | 16. B |
| 7. D | 17. B |
| 8. D | 18. D |
| 9. C | 19. D |
| 10. C | 20. A |

21. C
22. C
23. B
24. C
25. B

# EXAMINATION SECTION
# TEST 1

DIRECTIONS: Each question or incomplete statement is followed by several suggested answers or completions. Select the one that BEST answers the question or completes the Statement. *PRINT THE LETTER OF THE CORRECT ANSWER IN THE SPACE AT THE RIGHT.*

1. What type of pump has a diffusion *ring*?

    A. Centrifugal  B. Duplex double acting
    C. Helical gear  D. Spur gear

    1.\_\_\_\_

2. A cause of excessive oil consumption in an air compressor is

    A. oil with improper viscosity
    B. defective discharge valve
    C. oil level too high in oil sump
    D. loose unloader unit

    2.\_\_\_\_

3. How does cylinder oil compare with engine oil at engine room temperature? Cylinder oil

    A. is lighter in color
    B. has a higher viscosity
    C. has a lower viscosity
    D. is lighter when put in front of a light

    3.\_\_\_\_

4. On a boiler-feed centrifugal pump, to maintain a certain speed, 60 horsepower is used. To double that speed, so as to obtain double the output, how much horsepower is needed?

    A. 120    B. 240    C. 360    D. 480

    4.\_\_\_\_

5. The *slip* of a pump refers to

    A. lost motion on the steam slide valve
    B. leakage past the plunger on an outside packed pump
    C. recirculation of liquid from discharge side back to suction side
    D. clearance when piston is slipped inside cylinder

    5.\_\_\_\_

6. On a reciprocating vacuum pump, the diameter of the steam piston is _____ the liquid piston.

    A. larger than  B. smaller than
    C. the same size as  D. twice the diameter of

    6.\_\_\_\_

7. How many valves are there on the water end of a duplex double-acting feed pump?

    A. 8    B. 6    C. 4    D. 2

    7.\_\_\_\_

8. Which of the following would you find on a duplex pump?

   A. Springs and packing
   B. Gears and impeller
   C. Flywheel and crank
   D. Crankshaft and air chamber

9. The function of the air chamber on a duplex, double-acting pump is to

   A. prevent hammering
   B. increase capacity of pump
   C. aerate the water
   D. prevent cavitation

10. The valve discs on the water end of a duplex pump are USUALLY made of

    A. wood
    B. steel
    C. rubber
    D. cast iron

11. A direct-acting, duplex steam pump *short strokes* when it returns from overhaul. The PROBABLE cause is

    A. feed water too cold
    B. steam pressure too low
    C. steam valves not properly set
    D. water discharge pressure too high

12. A heavy duty pump is one which

    A. is designed for the pumping of heavy liquids
    B. pumps large quantities of water
    C. has a high thermal efficiency
    D. is made of extra heavy material for high head pressure

13. When a punch is used in making holes for rivets or boiler tubes, the diameter of the punch shall be _____ the desired hole.

    A. three-quarters of the diameter of
    B. slightly smaller than
    C. exactly the same size as
    D. slightly larger than

14. On a _____ pump, you would find a *volute*.

    A. reciprocating
    B. centrifugal
    C. jet
    D. direct-pressure

15. In starting a centrifugal boiler feed pump with 300 lbs. water pressure on the line, the valves should be set with suction _____ and discharge _____.

    A. open; open
    B. open; closed
    C. closed; closed
    D. closed; open

16. On a centrifugal boiler feed pump, the regulating valve functions to maintain

    A. speed constant
    B. pressure constant
    C. variable speed
    D. water level

17. With centrifugal pumps, the head varies directly as the 17.____

    A. speed
    B. speed squared
    C. speed cubed
    D. diameter squared

18. An intercooler is used on a 18.____

    A. compound engine
    B. two-stage air compressor
    C. two-stage turbine
    D. two-stage evactor

19. The unloader on an air compressor is provided for 19.____

    A. reducing pressure
    B. easy starting
    C. high-starting pressure
    D. reducing temperature

20. A duplex center outside a packed feed water pump has 20.____

    A. yoke rod
    B. two water plungers
    C. compound steam glands
    D. four water pistons

21. A centrifugal pump operates with a high suction lift, which would require _____ line. 21.____

    A. lift check at bottom of suction
    B. swing check in discharge
    C. stop valve in discharge
    D. lift check at top of suction

22. Diffuser vanes will MOST generally be found in a _____ pump. 22.____

    A. centrifugal turbine
    B. centrifugal volute
    C. rotary
    D. reciprocating

23. A sewer ejector would be located 23.____

    A. on the roof of a building
    B. in the basement
    C. in the sub-basement
    D. in the sewer

24. How many pots are there on a double-acting water pump? 24.____

    A. 1     B. 2     C. 3     D. 4

25. What is the amount of steam consumption of a simple, duplex steam pump, in lbs./H.P. hour? 25.____

    A. 5-20     B. 25-35     C. 50-90     D. 120-200

## KEY (CORRECT ANSWERS)

1. A
2. C
3. B
4. D
5. B

6. B
7. A
8. A
9. A
10. C

11. C
12. D
13. D
14. B
15. A

16. D
17. B
18. B
19. A
20. B

21. A
22. A
23. C
24. D
25. A

# TEST 2

DIRECTIONS: Each question or incomplete statement is followed by several suggested answers or completions. Select the one that BEST answers the question or completes the statement. *PRINT THE LETTER OF THE CORRECT ANSWER IN THE SPACE AT THE RIGHT.*

1. The type of valve on a duplex steam pump is   1.____

    A. sleeve
    B. piston
    C. D-slide valve
    D. poppet

2. The slide valve on a Knowles pump is operated by   2.____

    A. linkage attached to the piston rod
    B. rocker arm of opposite steam slide
    C. an auxiliary piston
    D. discharge water pressure

3. A duplex, double-acting pump with the valves properly adjusted will   3.____

    A. not start sometimes
    B. always start
    C. jig
    D. start when off dead center

4. If one valve stem of a duplex, double-acting pump broke, the pump would   4.____

    A. increase in speed
    B. run slower
    C. stop
    D. run on one side only

5. The diameter of the steam cylinders of an 18 x 16 x 24 duplex, direct-acting steam pump is _____ inches.   5.____

    A. 18
    B. 16
    C. 24
    D. 30

6. On a boiler feed pump, the   6.____

    A. steam cylinder is always larger than the water cylinder
    B. water cylinder is always larger than the steam cylinder
    C. cylinders are of equal size
    D. water discharge pipe is always larger than the suction pipe

7. Flax packing is used for   7.____

    A. steam end of pump
    B. water end of pump
    C. between flanges of pipe lines
    D. high temperature

8. Water is dripping out of the gland of a centrifugal pump used to pump feed water. You should   8.____

    A. renew the packing at the first opportunity
    B. pull up the gland as tight as possible with an ordinary 6 inch pipe wrench

93

C. pull up the gland just to the point where water does not leak out
D. do nothing

9. On the initial tightening of a jam-type gland on a boiler-feed water pump to stop excessive leakage, you would pull up alternately on the hexagonal nuts _____ turn.

   A. 1/6    B. 1/2    C. 3/4    D. 1 full

10. Diffuser vanes will MOST generally be found in a _____ pump.

    A. centrifugal turbine    B. centrifugal volute
    C. rotary                 D. reciprocating

11. If the consumption of lubricating oil in an air compressor is excessive, it is MOST likely due to

    A. using too high viscosity oil
    B. a defective discharge valve
    C. a loose unloader unit
    D. oil too high in sump

12. Which of the following statements is CORRECT about a Worthington steam-driven duplex double-acting boiler feed pump?

    A. Will always start in position in which it was stopped
    B. Will not start if stopped with one piston at extreme head end and other at dead center
    C. Speed is controlled by inertia type governor
    D. Dust of f must always be 25%

13. Centrifugal boiler feed pumps for large boilers with fluctuating loads are usually fitted with a system for recirculating or recycling.
    This is done to prevent

    A. excessive head pressure
    B. loss of suction
    C. excessing governor action
    D. overheating with consequent flashing and seizing of the pump

14. In the operation of a turbo-driven centrifugal pump, the delivery of the pump would PROPERLY be controlled by

    A. throttling the discharge
    B. throttling the suction
    C. using a bypass
    D. throttling the steam supply

15. Assume that it is necessary to pump 40 M.G.D. against a 65 ft. head.
    If the pump efficiency is 65%, the B.H.P. of this pump is MOST NEARLY

    A. 920    B. 700    C. 460    D. 176

16. Assume that a pump had to be shut down temporarily due to trouble which was first reported by an oiler.
    The one of the following entries in the log concerning this occurrence which is LEAST important is

    A. time of the shutdown
    B. period of time the pump was out of service
    C. cause of the trouble
    D. time the oiler came on shift

17. At sea level, the theoretical maximum distance, in feet, the water can be lifted by suction *only* is MOST NEARLY

    A. 12.00    B. 14.70    C. 33.57    D. 72.00

18. While a lubricating oil is in use, for good performance, its neutralization number should

    A. keep rising
    B. remain about the same
    C. be greater than 0.1
    D. be greater than 2.0

19. The parts of a large sewage pump that would MOST likely need repairs after the fewest number of hours of operation are the

    A. pump casings
    B. impellers
    C. wearing rings
    D. outboard bearings

20. Flexible coupling used to connect a pump to an electric motor valve is USUALLY rated in horsepower per

    A. 100 rpm of shaft
    B. 300 rpm of shaft
    C. square inch of shaft area
    D. inch of shaft diameter

## KEY (CORRECT ANSWERS)

| | | | |
|---|---|---|---|
| 1. | C | 11. | D |
| 2. | B | 12. | A |
| 3. | B | 13. | D |
| 4. | C | 14. | D |
| 5. | A | 15. | B |
| 6. | A | 16. | D |
| 7. | B | 17. | C |
| 8. | D | 18. | B |
| 9. | A | 19. | C |
| 10. | A | 20. | A |

# MECHANICAL APTITUDE
# TOOLS AND THEIR USE
# EXAMINATION SECTION
# TEST 1

DIRECTIONS: Each question or incomplete statement is followed by several suggested answers or completions. Select the one that BEST answers the question or completes the statement. *PRINT THE LETTER OF THE CORRECT ANSWER IN THE SPACE AT THE RIGHT.*

Questions 1-15.

DIRECTIONS: Questions 1 through 15 refer to the tools shown below. The numbers in the answers refer to the numbers beneath the tools. NOTE: These tools are NOT shown to scale.

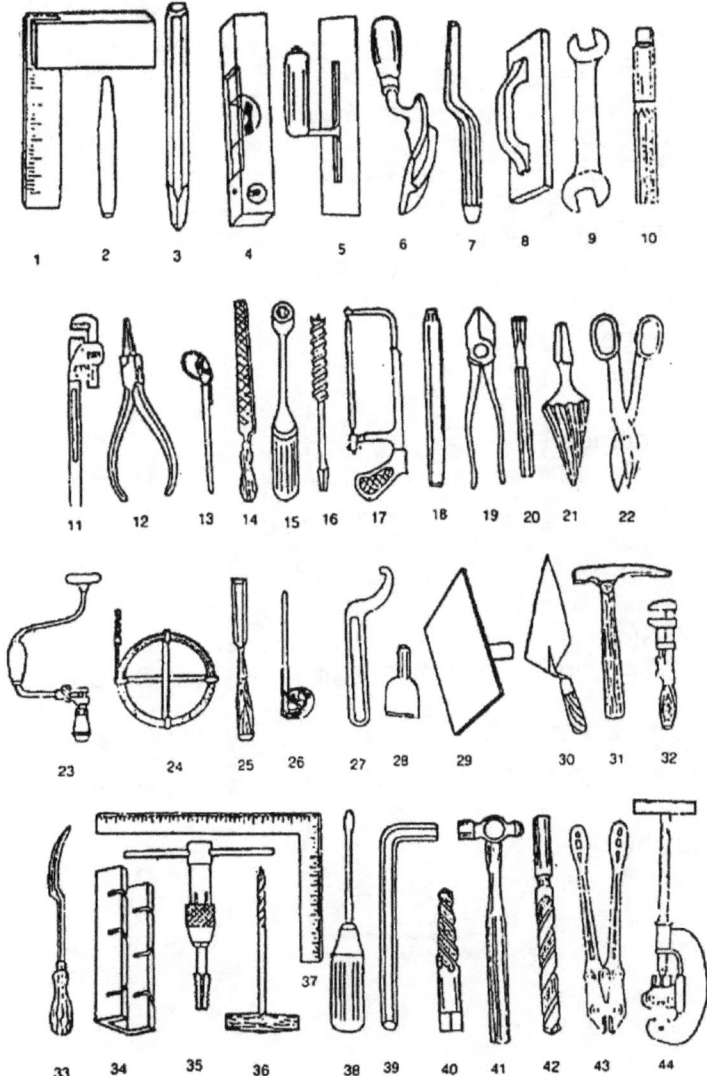

1. A "pipe reamer" is tool number
   A. 2　　　B. 10　　　C. 21　　　D. 24

2. A "mitre box" is tool number
   A. 1　　　B. 4　　　C. 25　　　D. 34

3. A "bolt cutter" is tool number
   A. 3　　　B. 25　　　C. 40　　　D. 43

4. The proper "drill bit" for wood is tool number
   A. 10　　　B. 16　　　C. 21　　　D. 40

5. A "ball peen" is tool number
   A. 20　　　B. 31　　　C. 33　　　D. 41

6. A "hawk" is tool number
   A. 5　　　B. 28　　　C. 29　　　D. 30

7. "Snips" is tool number
   A. 12　　　B. 19　　　C. 22　　　D. 43

8. A "bull point" is tool number
   A. 3　　　B. 7　　　C. 10　　　D. 20

9. An "open-end wrench" is tool number
   A. 9　　　B. 11　　　C. 15　　　D. 27

10. A "drift pin" is tool number
    A. 2　　　B. 3　　　C. 10　　　D. 40

11. A "pipe cutter" is tool number
    A. 17　　　B. 18　　　C. 28　　　D. 44

12. A "trowel" is tool number
    A. 6　　　B. 8　　　C. 28　　　D. 30

13. A "square" is tool number
    A. 4　　　B. 29　　　C. 34　　　D. 37

14. A "float" is tool number
    A. 8　　　B. 28　　　C. 29　　　D. 30

15. A "snake" is tool number
    A. 13　　　B. 24　　　C. 26　　　D. 36

## KEY (CORRECT ANSWERS)

| | | | | | |
|---|---|---|---|---|---|
| 1. | C | 6. | C | 11. | D |
| 2. | D | 7. | C | 12. | D |
| 3. | D | 8. | A | 13. | D |
| 4. | B | 9. | A | 14. | A |
| 5. | D | 10. | A | 15. | B |

# TEST 2

DIRECTIONS: Each question or incomplete statement is followed by several suggested answers or completions. Select the one that BEST answers the question or completes the statement. *PRINT THE LETTER OF THE CORRECT ANSWER IN THE SPACE AT THE RIGHT.*

1. The tool shown at the right is a
   A. countersink
   B. counterbore
   C. star drill
   D. burring reamer

   1._____

2. The saw shown at the right would be used to cut
   A. curved designs in thin wood
   B. strap iron
   C. asphalt tiles to fit against walls
   D. soft lead pipe

   2._____

3. The tool shown at the right is a
   A. float
   B. finishing trowel
   C. hawk
   D. roofing seamer

   3._____

4. The hammer shown to the right would be used by a
   A. carpenter
   B. bricklayer
   C. tinsmith
   D. plumber

   4._____

5. When drilling into a steel plate, the MOST likely cause for the breaking of a drill bit is
   A. too low a drill speed
   B. excessive cutting oil lubricant
   C. too much drill pressure
   D. using a bit with a dull point

   5._____

6. Of the following, the MOST important advantage of a ratchet wrench over an open-end wrench is that the ratchet wrench
   A. can be used in a more limited space
   B. measures the torque applied
   C. will not strip the threads of a bolt
   D. is available for all sizes of hex bolts

   6._____

7. The tool that holds the die when threading pipe is generally called a
   A. vise        B. stock        C. yoke        D. coupling

   7._____

100

8. A fitting used to join a small pipe at right angles to the middle of a large pie is called a
   A. union  B. coupling  C. cap  D. reducing tee

9. Gaskets are commonly used between the flanges of large pipe joints to
   A. make a leakproof connection
   B. provide for expansion
   C. provide space for assembly
   D. adjust for poor alignment

10. The pipe fitting that should be used to connect a 1" pipe to a 1½" valve is called a
    A. reducing coupling
    B. nipple
    C. bushing
    D. union

11. The part of a drill press which is used to hold the drill bit is called a
    A. chuck  B. collar  C. bit  D. vise

12. When grinding a flat chisel, it is GOOD practice to keep the chisel moving across the face of the grinding wheel in order to prevent
    A. grooving of the wheel
    B. burning of the chisel tip
    C. the wheel from vibrating
    D. the wheel from cracking

13. In order to determine if a surface is *truly* horizontal, it should be checked with a
    A. carpenters square
    B. plumb bob
    C. steel rule
    D. spirit level

14. A gauge of a nail indicates the
    A. length of the shank
    B. diameter of the head
    C. thickness of the head
    D. diameter of the shank

15. A tool can be used BOTH for scribing regular arcs and also for transferring dimensions is the
    A. trammel
    B. protractor
    C. scriber
    D. combination square

16. The devices for clamping sheet metal in place on a squaring shear are the
    A. clamps  B. hold-downs  C. guides  D. square

17. When a hacksaw is used to cut out sheet metal, the BEST blade to use is one with _____ teeth per inch.
    A. 14  B. 18  C. 24  D. 32

18. A tool which may be attached to a drill press and used to cut circles of 2½" diameter or larger in sheet metal is the
    A. twist drill  B. circular saw  C. reamer  D. hole saw

19. A versatile hand tool that can be used for a variety of sheet metalwork jobs such as bucking up rivet heads, straightening kinks in formed metal, forming seals, etc. is the
    A. hand dolly
    B. universal iron worker
    C. cupping tool
    D. set hammer

20. To make certain two points separated by a vertical distance of 8 feet are in perfect vertical alignment, it would be BEST to use a(n)
    A. surface gage
    B. height gage
    C. protractor
    D. plumb bob

21. A claw hammer is PROPERLY used for
    A. driving a cold chisel
    B. driving brads
    C. setting rivets
    D. flattening a ½" metal bar

22. It would NOT be good practice to tighten a 1" hexagon nut with a(n) _____ wrench.
    A. monkey
    B. 1" fixed open-end
    C. adjustable open-end
    D. stillson

23. Lock washers are used PRINCIPALLY with _____ screws.
    A. machine    B. wood    C. self-tapping    D. lag

24. Toggle bolts are MOST appropriate for use to fasten conduit clamps to a
    A. steel column
    B. concrete wall
    C. hollow tile wall
    D. brick wall

25. If a 10-24 by ¾" machine screw is not available, the screw which could be MOST easily modified to use in an emergency is a
    A. 10-24 by ½"
    B. 12-24 by ¾"
    C. 10-2 by 1½"
    D. 8-24 by ¾"

26. Of the following tools, the one that should be used to cut thin-wall metal tubing is the
    A. reamer    B. plier    C. hacksaw    D. broach

27. A wrench that can be used to tighten a nut to a specified tightness is a _____ wrench.
    A. bonney    B. spud    C. torque    D. adjustable

28. The one of the following that will MOST likely show a "mushroomed" head is a
    A. cold chisel
    B. file cleaner
    C. screwdriver blade
    D. ratchet

29. A tool that is used to bend pipe is the
    A. lintel    B. hickey    C. collet    D. brace

30. Before drilling a hole in a steel plate, an indentation should be made with a          30._____
    A. center punch    B. nail         C. drill bit       D. pin punch

## KEY (CORRECT ANSWERS)

| | | |
|---|---|---|
| 1. D | 11. A | 21. B |
| 2. A | 12. A | 22. D |
| 3. A | 13. D | 23. A |
| 4. B | 14. D | 24. C |
| 5. C | 15. A | 25. C |
| 6. A | 16. B | 26. C |
| 7. B | 17. D | 27. C |
| 8. D | 18. D | 28. A |
| 9. A | 19. A | 29. B |
| 10. C | 20. D | 30. A |